AUTISM SPECTRUM DISORDER

Lorna Selfe

ALL THAT MATTERS

ALL THAT MATTERS

First published in Great Britain in 2013 by Hodder & Stoughton. An Hachette UK company.

First published in US in 2013 by The McGraw-Hill Companies, Inc.

This edition published 2013

British Library Cataloguing in Publication Data: a catalogue record for this title is available from the British Library.

Library of Congress Catalog Card Number: on file.

10 9 8 7 6 5 4 3 2 1

Typeset by Cenveo® Publisher Services.

Printed and bound in Great Britain by CPI Group (UK) Ltd., Croydon, CR0 4YY.

Hodder & Stoughton policy is to use papers that are natural, renewable and recyclable products and made from wood grown in sustainable forests. The logging and manufacturing processes are expected to conform to the environmental regulations of the country of origin.

Hodder & Stoughton Ltd

338 Euston Road

London NW1 3BH

www.hodder.co.uk

Contents

Introduction

This book is written at a watershed in our conceptualization of autism spectrum disorders (ASD). Diagnosis, until 2013, has largely depended on meeting the criteria set out in the Diagnostic and Statistical Manual (DSM) Version 4 of the American Psychiatric Association (APA) and the International Classification of Diseases (ICD) Version 10 of the World Health Organization (WHO). Both manuals are being extensively reorganized, in joint collaboration, and the DSM Version 5 was published in May 2013. The ICD-11 will follow shortly. The criteria for diagnosis have been revised and Asperger's syndrome has been subsumed under the ASD umbrella and three levels of severity have been introduced. Changes in diagnostic criteria will lead to changes in assessments. The significance of the changes is discussed in Chapter 3 and the three levels of severity are used to describe interventions in Chapters 5, 6, 7 and 8.

While there is now one diagnostic umbrella term, namely ASD, there is growing acknowledgement that ASD is not one single condition with one single cause. It is a number of different conditions all showing similar behavioural features. There is a great deal of agreement about these core behavioural impairments and there is general agreement about its neurological basis. At the same time, genetic research is having its own paradigm shift which will impact on ASD research. There is now evidence of a complex interaction between genetic and environmental factors in triggering ASD. The evidence for environmental triggers, brain abnormalities, neurological dysfunction and genetic factors is presented in Chapter 9. We now have some robust psychological theories about underlying cognitive deficits in autism, which will be discussed in Chapter 10.

As a clinician I have been involved with assessment, diagnosis and educational interventions with children with ASD and these are likely to be the book's preoccupations. As such this book is written for parents, teachers and general readers rather than for the academic and scientific community. References to academic sources have largely been omitted in the text. However, details of these can be found in the Further reading at the end of the book. The references are arranged in the order they appear in the chapter, so the purposeful reader should be able to link the text to the reference. Also, 20 Key Books used in the text are referenced in the list of 100 Ideas. The book is primarily concerned with ASD in childhood because the focus of most research is on causation, assessment and diagnosis which necessarily occur in the early, formative years. Nevertheless, the text is relevant to an understanding of adolescents and adults with ASD.

Towards an understanding of autism

I don't know what autism is, and wonder whether anybody does. Absurdly loose definition and a shocking lack of diagnostic rigour threaten to rob terms such as 'autistic' or 'Asperger's' of any useful medical meaning. Yet in the sloppy sense in which the diagnosis is sprayed around these days, I suspect that we are all autistic but some of us have learned to hide it better than others.

Matthew Parris

ALL THAT
MATTERS

The journalist Matthew Parris, writing in *The Times* in August 2013, reflects a widely held confusion and scepticism about autism and Asperger's syndrome. This book will endeavour to answer the issues he raises. The history of ASD is relatively short. It is the product of comparatively young sciences, neurology, psychology and psychiatry, but to have a child who suffers from autism is to leave parents in no doubt about its special status and reality.

▶ The process of socialization

From earliest history human beings have lived in families and social groups to enhance their mutual survival. Of all the animals it is humans who have to nurture and protect their young for the longest period of time. The child must remain within the family structure for safety and security and could not survive without such support. The family into which a child is born normally retains control and nurture of the young until the child reaches adolescence after which it becomes possible to become independent. The behaviour of the young is effectively shaped by membership of a family unit.

Margaret Thatcher famously stated in 1987, 'There is no such thing as society'. This statement was in the context of praising individualism, free enterprise and the ethics of capitalism. It is relevant in the context of issues relating to ASD because it points out a simple truth that in a social world that extols individualism we can overlook the fact that human beings are profoundly social animals. It is the failure of normal responses to everyday social events that is the essence of autism. ASD is characterized by persistent impairment in social communication and interaction as well as restricted and repetitive patterns of behaviour.

Lev Vygotsky, the Russian psychologist (1896–1934), was under no illusion about the role of society when he described child development in his book as a 'mind in society'. His theories stress the fundamental role of social interaction in the development of thinking and cognition. Vygotsky says learning and development result from a dynamic interaction between the child and care-givers. Only as a member of a social community can the child come to make sense of the world. Unconsciously, the adult models behaviours and provides verbal instructions for the child. Children learn to understand these actions and words then internalize the information, using it to guide or regulate their own behaviour.

Vygotsky noted that humans, unlike animals, can act on and change their environment in remarkable ways. Culturally produced sign systems such as language and writing transform social life and are the source of reasoning and thinking. Children learn verbal labels from care-givers which relate to objects and actions. The moment that the child recognizes signs and words have meanings that relate to objects and activities in the real world is 'the greatest discovery in the child's life'. For Vygotsky the development of speech is 'the very essence of complex human behaviour'. The child can now master the environment with the help of communication with other humans. He concluded that social interaction involving language is essential for intelligent action.

▶ The nature and importance of language

It is no coincidence that the impairments involved in ASD encompass difficulties with language and communication because language is essentially a social phenomenon. This idea of the social origins of language was explored by the philosopher Ludwig Wittgenstein (1889–1951). He discussed the relationship between thought and language and how language develops in a social context. Wittgenstein proposed that words and language developed as a negotiation between people about external reality. This includes objects that exist in the environment and the actions that are performed in it.

Sociability is fundamental to what it means to be human and to our very existence and survival. The impetus for social communication is with us from our earliest days. Infants are born with a set of abilities which allow them to interact with their care-givers to ensure their survival; smiling, gurgling, crying are the basic forms of social interaction where the child indicates a need and the carer responds. Babies are totally dependent and if they cannot relate to other human beings they are in danger. Non-verbal interactions develop into language systems in an ever more elaborate social dance between child and care-giver and child and the wider family group. Individuals pass through stages of growth and development from childhood to adolescence, until they are eventually able to exist independently. Adults choose their own social network. But whichever new group a person joins, the rules, norms and values must be understood and adhered to in order to be accepted into the group.

There are instructive cases of feral children. They are children who have been deprived of adult human contact from a very young age, and who have no experience of human care or parental love and affection. A famous example is that of a boy who was discovered in 1799 in the forests near Aveyron, in France. He was thought to be between 10 and 12 years old; he had no speech and behaved like a wild animal. He was taken to Paris for assessment by Dr Jean Itard, and named Victor. In descriptions made of him at the time, it was noted that he spent much time rocking (a characteristic of severe autism). He made little progress and despite every care and assistance, he learned only two utterances: 'milk' and a cry, 'Oh God'. He mastered only a few basic menial tasks during his subsequent life, and died at the age of about 40. What is particularly significant is that these rare, feral children who have apparently had little or no socialization, never master language when rescued and behave in an autistic manner. The research around the phenomenon of feral children has assisted in developing theories about the evolution of language and socialization.

▶ What it means to have ASD

Social and emotional 'intelligence' enable individuals to partake in society and belong to a range of diverse groups. A child who cannot relate to others, who cannot make friendships, cannot read the minds and gestures of others and who lacks the ability to develop complex language will have many challenges in partaking in society effectively and independently.

While it is easy to understand what it must be like to be deaf or blind by covering our ears or eyes, it is not so easy to understand what it means to have impairments in social comprehension and communication. Nevertheless, having the normal faculties of social comprehension and social interaction is as important as being able to see and hear. Impairments suffered by those with ASD are potentially devastating. Social communication is fundamental to what it means to be human and just as there are pathways in the brain involving hearing and vision, there are others, as yet not fully designated, which are involved in social comprehension and social interaction.

The key problem in autism is a deficit in the ability to relate to other human beings. It manifests itself in difficulties in the first three years of life with socialization. Babies with ASD often fail to look at their parents, share their eye gaze, cue in and join activities (known as joint attention). They fail to respond to back-and-forth lap games or follow their parent's pointing finger. They fail to understand or use body language such as nodding, wagging a finger or shrugging shoulders (types of non-verbal communication). They appear uninvolved and indifferent to facial expression and the emotions of others (lacking empathy). Secondary to problems of socialization are those of developing language. Put simply, if the natural impetus to interact is not present, if there are problems with joint attention and non-verbal communication, then the infant is unlikely to imitate and acquire a vocabulary of words shared by the common community around them. Children with ASD frequently show considerable delays in acquiring words, sentences and language, both receptive and expressive.

A further consequence of social isolation and impairments in language and communication is that the child will retreat into his or her own world of self-stimulation, repetitive and restricted behaviours. The child will occupy his or her time with isolated pursuits such as lining up toys, spinning wheels, collecting objects, shredding paper, rocking and hand flapping. The usual social demands often create a great deal of anxiety in the child, so that such occupations and insistence on routines serve to reduce human social interaction and anxiety. Problems with language development and with repetitive, restricted patterns of behaviour are, therefore, seen as an inevitable consequence of the fundamental difficulty with social comprehension and a deficit in the natural inclination to engage with others.

▶ Key features of ASD and overview

ASD is a neurodevelopmental condition possibly affecting as many as one in 100 people. It is regarded as being pervasive because it affects so many functions and is life-long. The key diagnostic features of the disorder are problems with social understanding, communication and repetitive and restricted behaviours. These difficulties usually result from a number of different genetic and environmental factors leading to similar behavioural features. Children who could be described as autistic vary widely in cognitive ability, in presenting symptoms and underlying genetic and neurological status. There is no one homogeneous underlying cause, hence the notion of a range of disorders with some common defining features. Mary Coleman and Christopher Gillberg are two experts in the field who stated in 2011 that 'the autisms represent a group of conditions with multiple aetiologies'. The modern view is that there are a number of disorders under the ASD umbrella all linked by common behavioural features. The subgroups are only just being recognized and identified. The term spectrum is, therefore, used to acknowledge this diversity.

People with ASD vary widely depending on the severity of the condition, the age of the person and developmental level. This continuum can run from one extreme, those with severe disabilities, unable to look after themselves, to the other, where someone has unusual behaviours but can exist perfectly well in the general community. It is regularly said that, when you have met one person with autism you have met **one** person with autism. Every child diagnosed with ASD is at a different point along the spectrum and may be very different from another person with the same diagnosis.

There is no simple medical test for ASD although our understanding of the underlying biological processes producing ASD behaviours is proceeding rapidly. The diagnosis is usually undertaken by a multi-professional team comprising a psychiatrist (who is medically trained), a psychologist (who studies behaviour and brain function) and a speech therapist (who has training in speech and language disorders). Diagnosis usually includes observations of the child and interviews with the parents. The diagnostic features are laid out in the manuals of the APA and the WHO.

Autism is a puzzling and distressing condition but, in terms of medical science, relatively recently recognized and defined. The variation between children along the spectrum and the discovery of multiple genetic causes adds to the confusion. The process of investigating and understanding ASD is accelerating and a great deal of research is being undertaken. Currently, we are going through an upheaval in definition and diagnosis but it is very likely that the next decades will prove to be highly productive ones and breakthroughs will be made as research progresses. Although it is distressing for those involved in the lives of a person with autism when communication and understanding are difficult, there are many reasons to be optimistic about the future: new interventions are being developed and refined all the time, training for teachers and others in assisting pupils with ASD has vastly improved, knowledge of the causes of ASD and diagnosis has been deepening, more positive attitudes and public awareness of the condition has been growing and there are examples of autistic people who have become eminent having achieved success as artists, musicians or as academics.

History and definitions of ASD

[ASD] is best conceptualised as a biologically determined set of behaviours that occur with varying presentation and severity, probably as the result of varying causes.

Goldstein, Naglieri and Ozonoff

ALL THAT MATTERS

▶ Classical autism

These days autism is seen as a neurological disorder as described by Goldstein and colleagues. Its original conception was as a psychiatric disorder. 'Early Infantile Autism' was first described by Leo Kanner, a psychiatrist working in the USA, in 1943. Of course autism has always existed and there are reports from previous centuries about the behaviour of patients in psychiatric institutions which resembled symptoms which are now recognized as severe autism. In the 19th century, many children who are now seen as having ASD were often diagnosed with 'childhood schizophrenia'; this persisted into the 1950s. In his initial research, Kanner identified a group of 11 children who were characterized by abnormal behaviours, which he described as:

1 A profound lack of affective contact with other people

2 An anxiously obsessive desire for the preservation of sameness

3 A fascination with objects which are handled with skill

4 Mutism or a kind of language that does not seem to intend to serve interpersonal communication

5 Good cognitive potential manifested in those who can speak, by feats of memory

Subsequently, classical autism has come to be regarded as a severe disorder marked by significant cognitive and communication problems. These include major deficiencies with social interaction, delays in or lack of language and repetitive and restricted behaviours. People with classical autism may require supervision and support all their lives.

▲ Leo Kanner (1894–1981) Hans Asperger (1906–1980)

▶ Asperger's syndrome

Someone with a diagnosis of Asperger's syndrome may not show delays in language development. In this sense it is a more subtle disorder and affected individuals will often only appear to be eccentric or unusual in their behaviour. Hans Asperger's pioneering paper was published in German in 1944. He was a child psychiatrist working in Vienna. He identified and described a very similar group of children to Kanner; however, his paper was largely overlooked in the post-war period. In his descriptions, Asperger's children were generally older and scored higher on IQ tests than those described by Kanner. They had normal language development but with pedantic speech, odd behaviour, difficulties with non-verbal communication and were excessively clumsy.

Asperger's syndrome is characterized by:

- Severe impairment of reciprocal social interaction
- Evidence of all-absorbing, narrow interests
- The need for strict routines in day-to-day life
- Speech and language problems but without delayed development
- Non-verbal communication problems
- Motor clumsiness

There is an overlap between the descriptions of the two syndromes but Uta Frith, renowned expert in the field, claimed, 'On all the major features of autism Kanner and Asperger are in agreement'.

Asperger's syndrome is less severe than classical autism. Most people can interpret the feelings and motives of others from their body language and facial expression. Those diagnosed as having Asperger's syndrome have difficulty in making such interpretations and in reading social cues. Some individuals with the syndrome avoid making eye contact, whereas others may stare uncomfortably: both can affect normal social interactions. They lack the ability to see the subtleties involved in social discourse whereby people normally react to their interpretations of the behaviour of others as a guide to their own. Consequently, their own patterns of behaviour may be regarded by others as eccentric or odd, which in a school situation can lead to bullying and isolation. While those with Asperger's syndrome may face obstacles in social relationships, many adjust to the challenges and live effective, independent lives.

It was not until 1981 that Lorna Wing, a paediatrician noted for her work on autism, rediscovered Asperger's original work and brought it to the attention of the medical and academic fraternity. Some clinicians maintain that Asperger's is a separate condition from autism. Others argue that there should be no dividing line between 'high-functioning' autism and Asperger's syndrome and both groups benefit from the same intervention techniques. It would appear that the latter group has won the debate since Asperger's syndrome has now been dropped from DSM-5.

Asperger's syndrome, classical autism and some other pathological conditions were grouped together under the category of Pervasive Developmental Disorder in DSM-4. There was the possibility of a further diagnostic category of Pervasive Developmental Disorder: Not Otherwise Specified (PDD-NOS) which was used for conditions that resembled ASD but did not meet the full criteria necessary for a positive diagnosis. These disorders were then grouped by the National Autistic Society (NAS) among others, collectively, under the heading Autistic Spectrum Disorders. More will be said about the changed situation when DSM-5 is discussed in the next chapter.

▶ Triad of impairments

As autism came to be universally recognized and research proceeded, a pattern of three areas of impairments emerged. This became the triad of impairments enshrined in DSM-4. Features related to all three areas had to be present for a positive diagnosis:

- **Qualitative impairment in social interaction.** For example, marked impairment in eye gaze, and non-verbal behaviour; failure to develop peer relationships; and a lack of shared enjoyment, interests and emotional reciprocity.

- **Qualitative impairment in communication.** Such as, delayed and deviant language development; marked impairment in the ability to use conversation; stereotyped and repetitive use of language; and lack of make-believe and imaginative play.

- **Restricted, repetitive and stereotyped patterns of behaviour, interests and activities.** For example, obsessions with objects and certain activities; insistence on routines and rituals; and stereotyped and repetitive motor mannerisms such as hand flapping.

▶ The prevalence of ASD

Diagnosis of ASD has been rising steadily over the past 20 years. The prevalence figure in the UK in the 1960s was estimated to be six children in 10,000. In 1979 Lorna Wing and Judith Gould reported on an epidemiological study in Camberwell. This confirmed an incidence of about five in 10,000 for children with classical autism (the study was conducted before Asperger's syndrome had been recognized). However, they suggested that there was a further, larger group of children with delayed and disordered language and social development. In the 1980s, the inclusion of Asperger's syndrome widened the field and this new category was added to classical autism. By the mid-1990s a figure as high as 58 in 10,000, or almost six in every 1,000 children, was regularly quoted. Currently, the NAS suggests that the incidence is about one child in 100 in the UK, derived from several sources. The incidence in the USA, as reported by Robin Hansen and Sally Rogers in 2013, is one in 88 children, while official statistics from Italy report an incidence of eight in 10,000 and a study in Japan reported a prevalence of 21 in 10,000. This range of incidence shows the variability in applying diagnostic definitions in different countries. More will be said about this in the next chapter.

In all economically developed countries the incidence has been rising but few commentators have suggested that we are in the grip of an epidemic. The notion of what constitutes autism has widened to include people who are otherwise mildly affected. Also our understanding of a spectrum of disorders which included Asperger's syndrome, with common core features, has improved, together with diagnostic acumen. Studies have also indicated that children who were once diagnosed as 'mentally retarded' have increasingly been classified more appropriately as having ASD. This has been labelled as the 'diagnostic substitution effect'. Concerns are now being expressed about the possible overdiagnosis of ASD. For example, Jack Nagliari notes that some of the diagnostic instruments are not well standardized. He claims that there is over-reliance on parental reports. They can be overly concerned due to intense media preoccupation with the issues of ASD.

▶ ASD today

Following a long period of research, debate and controversy, the revision of DSM-4 was published in

May 2013 as DSM-5. The categories subsumed under the heading Pervasive Developmental Disorders (including Asperger's syndrome) in DSM-4 were merged under one heading, Autism Spectrum Disorder. This is classified under the heading Neurodevelopmental Disorders and a delineation based on the severity of symptoms was instituted. The triad of impairments became a dyad as follows:

- Persistent deficits in social communication and social interaction across multiple contexts

- Restricted, repetitive patterns of behaviour, interests or activities.

A new category of Social (Pragmatic) Communication Disorder was added which is defined as 'Persistent difficulties with verbal and non-verbal communication' (see DSM-5). It is differentiated from ASD by the absence of restricted and repetitive behaviours and is characterized by difficulties with verbal and non-verbal communication that cannot be explained by low cognitive ability.

Diagnostic and Statistical Manual of Mental Disorders (DSM- 5)

ALL THAT
MATTERS

Professor Simon Baron-Cohen, Director of the Autism Research Centre in Cambridge, describes the DSM as:

The book that sits on the desk of every psychiatrist throughout the world and that psychiatrists consult to classify all 'mental illnesses'.

The DSM is the manual used by clinicians to diagnose and classify mental disorders. It was first published in 1952 and has been revised every 15 years or so to reflect the evolution of knowledge in psychiatry. The fifth edition was published in 2013. The APA has proposed new diagnostic criteria for autism for this edition. The APA is an organization whose members are mainly psychiatrists. They are responsible for conducting research into mental illnesses, including childhood disorders and ASD, and for producing diagnostic criteria.

The changes reflect the work of a team of psychiatrists, psychologists and academics supported by more than a decade of intensive study and analysis. Working parties on the various components of the manual have consulted colleagues in other countries and held international conferences and workshops. The conclusions have been published and have been made available for consultation as the process has progressed. (The DSM-5 debate can be read online). The proposal by the DSM-5 Neurodevelopmental Working Group recommended a new category, ASD, which would incorporate several previously separate diagnoses, including Autistic Disorder and Asperger's

Disorder. The others being three rare disorders: childhood disintegrative disorder, Rett's syndrome and PDD-NOS.

The rationale for the proposed changes asserted that symptoms of these five disorders represent a continuum and it is difficult to discern clear subgroups within this spectrum because features are so variable. As well as diagnosing the individual's overall status in terms of difficulties with social communication and restricted and repetitive behaviours, the proposed criteria for ASD specify a range of severity. The DSM-5 distinguishes between three levels of severity which can be identified by the clinician. The severity markers are as follows:

Severity level	Social communication	Restricted, repetitive behaviours
Level 3 – Requiring very substantial support. *Previously Classical Autism or Autistic Disorder (DSM-4)*	Severe deficits in verbal and non-verbal social communication skills cause severe impairments in functioning, very limited initiation of social interaction and minimal response from social overtures from others.	Inflexibility of behaviour, extreme difficulty in coping with change, or other restricted/repetitive behaviours markedly interfere with functioning in all spheres. Great distress/difficulty changing focus or action.
Level 2 – Requiring substantial support	Marked deficits in verbal and non-verbal social communication skills; social impairments apparent even with supports in place; limited initiation of social interactions and reduced or abnormal response to social overtures from others.	Inflexibility of behaviour, difficulty coping with change, or other restricted/repetitive behaviours appear frequently enough to be obvious to the casual observer and interfere with functioning in a variety of contexts. Distress or difficulty changing focus or action.

| Level 1 – Requiring support. *Previously mainly Asperger's Syndrome or Asperger's Disorder DSM-4* NB: Comments in italics are not in DSM-5 | Without support in place deficits in social communication cause noticeable impairments. Difficulty initiating social interaction, and clear examples of atypical or unsuccessful responses to social overtures from others. May appear to have decreased interest in social interactions. | Inflexibility of behaviour causes significant interference in functioning in one or more contexts. Difficulty switching between activities. Problems of organization and planning hamper independence. |

DSM-5 proponents claim that the proposed criteria will lead to more accurate diagnosis and will help teachers and therapists design better treatment interventions for children. It has been suggested that the DSM-5 criteria will improve the sensitivity and specificity of the diagnosis. Another important problem was that the previous diagnostic criteria tended not to be consistently applied across different clinics and centres and indeed across different cultures.

The DSM-5 criteria were tested in real-life clinical field trials. Field testing of the proposed criteria for ASD did not indicate that there will be any change in the number of patients receiving care in treatment centres, but it is claimed that more accurate diagnoses can lead to more focused treatment. The DSM-5 also states that people who already had a diagnosis of Autistic Disorder, Asperger's syndrome, Childhood Disintegrative Disorder or PDD-NOS should be regarded as meeting criteria for a diagnosis of ASD.

The NAS in the UK has summarized the further changes outlined below, which they regard as positive.

▶ Sensory behaviours are included in the criteria for the first time, under the 'restricted, repetitive patterns of behaviours' descriptors.

▶ The emphasis during diagnosis will change from giving a name to the condition to identifying all the needs someone has and how these affect their life.

▶ 'Dimensional elements' have been introduced which give an indication of how much someone's condition affects them. This will help to identify how much support an individual needs.

▶ Criticisms of the new diagnostic criteria and single diagnostic label

The fact that a distinction between classical autism and Asperger's syndrome was likely to be dropped in favour of one overarching label was known well ahead of publication of DSM-5. This occasioned protests in both the USA and in the UK. There was concern from those with a diagnosis of Asperger's Disorder and their parents that their condition would be marginalized or unrecognized and that they would lose entitlements to benefits despite reassurances that this would not be the case.

In a study published in October 2012 in the *American Journal of Psychiatry*, the case records of 4,453 children previously diagnosed with a pervasive developmental disorder using DSM-4 were reviewed in light of the outcomes. Some children had been incorrectly diagnosed with ASD. Based on these records, the researchers applied the new DSM-5 criteria to identify children with an ASD. The authors found that using the proposed new criteria they identified 91 per cent of those previously diagnosed under the DSM-4 system. Fewer children were incorrectly diagnosed using DSM-5. The children who would have lost their diagnosis under the new criteria did so mainly because their social impairments were not severe enough to meet DSM-5 criteria. The report did not include adults, and it remains unclear how the proposed changes will affect them.

In the UK the NAS has also discussed the changes. Although it has stated that its general view is a positive one it has also raised some concerns.

- The NAS believes that social interaction and communication problems are separate issues although they are combined in the new criteria. They prefer the old triad of impairments.

- Another major concern is the new diagnosis of Social (Pragmatic) Communication Disorder. This would be given when someone exhibits the social communication and interaction deficits of an ASD diagnosis, but does not show restricted or repetitive patterns of behaviour. People with such difficulties often have restricted or repetitive behaviours and interests, but have been able to mask them, particularly where someone is more able intellectually. The NAS claims that this group is actually a subgroup of people on the autism spectrum. It is their view that, 'When the aim of DSM-5 is to avoid having autism sub-groups, we do not believe it is helpful to have created this additional diagnosis of social communication disorder'.

DSM-5 collapses the distinction between social communication and social interaction. There is a strong argument that the addition of a new diagnosis of Social Communication Disorder runs against this logic. It may be that the inclusion of this category, under the general heading of Language Disorder, is an attempt to move a group of children who would have been diagnosed with ASD to this domain. This would resurrect the old concept of pragmatic/semantic language disorder which existed in earlier conceptions of language disorder.

In the context of wider concerns about labelling and diagnosing ASD, debate is inevitable. There are those who challenge the use of psychiatric labels on the basis that they can be used to present human reactions to adverse circumstances as a medical condition. Schizophrenia, for example, could be viewed as a reaction to intolerable circumstances rather than as an illness. Proponents of the DSM-5 believe that without labels and categories there can be no dialogue and real clinical and social problems cannot be addressed. DSM-5 is at least an attempt to move towards an ever more effective underlying classification system.

The next version of the ICD (ICD-11) is due to be published in 2015. The current one is very similar to DSM-4. The WHO said that it will consider the changes made in DSM-5 and that the aim is to align ICD with DSM as closely as possible, but their descriptions are often slightly different. At present, there is no definitive information of any plans to change the label of Asperger's syndrome in the new edition of ICD although most professionals think it likely that ICD-11 will follow the DSM-5 in this change. It is possible that the ICD-11, despite hope for harmonization, will ultimately not follow the lead of the DSM-5 with regard to ASD, and it is conceivable that this could cause immense confusion in the professions of psychiatry and psychology in Europe and the USA. A diagnosis of Asperger's syndrome will not be made in the USA in future but it is possible that it may continue to be made in Europe.

The assessment and diagnosis of ASD

In his review of assessment of ASD, Jack Nagliari says,

The better the tool, the more valid and reliable the decisions, the more useful the information obtained and the better the services that are eventually provided.

▶ Assessment of ASD

Most children with ASD have a degree of intellectual disability (ID) and about half will have moderate and severe intellectual impairment. For this reason the proper assessment of ASD will usually include an assessment of the child's cognitive abilities. Many of the characteristic features of ASD are developmentally sensitive. For example, lining up objects is typical behaviour of children at the stage before symbolic play emerges; reversing and substituting pronouns (e.g. 'Me do it') and echoing words and phrases are common in the early stages of language development. Therefore, the diagnosis of ASD should always be seen in the context of the child's age and overall cognitive and intellectual development.

Cognitive abilities are usually assessed using a standardized test. The most thoroughly researched of these, such as the British Abilities Scale 3 (BAS-3) or the Wechsler Intelligence Test for Children, Version 4 (WISC-4), have a number of subtests probing a range of different abilities. The child will either be above average, average or below average compared to the scores obtained by a large sample of children of the same age. A profile of scores is obtained revealing the child's strengths and weaknesses and an overall ability score can be computed if necessary. It could be argued that all children with ASD have a degree of learning difficulties since there are subtests on verbal abilities and comprehension and substantial weaknesses in these areas are part of the diagnostic criteria. The WISC-4 and the BAS-3 are founded on an assumption that there is one overarching factor called intelligence and an IQ score has some meaning.

Howard Gardner's theory of intelligence is, however, much more useful in considering the cognitive ability of people with ASD. He suggested that there are many forms of intelligence which are relatively independent of one another. His multi-factorial model has seven components.

Intelligence type	Capability and perception
Linguistic	Words and language
Logical-Mathematical	Logic and numbers
Musical	Music, sound, rhythm
Bodily-Kinaesthetic	Body movement control
Spatial-Visual	Images and space
Interpersonal	Other people's feelings
Intrapersonal	Self-awareness

People with ASD can frequently show considerable strengths and weaknesses. A few rare individuals with autism are termed 'autistic savants' and have very special skills particularly with music, calendar calculations and perspective drawing. People with ASD typically have a particular strength with spatial/visual intelligence (exemplified by the ability to do jigsaw puzzles and construct models). They have particular weaknesses with linguistic and interpersonal intelligence, such as comprehending other people's feelings.

Knowledge and understanding of autism has developed rapidly. It is now agreed that ASD does not imply one underlying genetic or neurological condition, rather it is a description of a range of behaviours that have been shown to co-exist. If social communication and social interaction are impaired then the child is likely to retreat from aversive interactions into activities which are repetitive, ritualistic and all-absorbing.

▶ Diagnosis

There are no medical tests for the disorder although, increasingly, neurological and genetic analyses are helping to elucidate underlying abnormalities and subtypes of the spectrum of disorders. Techniques for producing images of the brain and examining brain functioning include: Computerized Tomography (CT), Magnetic Resonance scanning (MRI), Positron Emission Tomography scanning (PET) and Diffusion Tensor Tracking.

Over the last 20 years, the principal protocols, DSM-4 and ICD-10, have dominated diagnosis and conceptualization. The most highly regarded assessment instruments used in the UK employ DSM-4 and ICD-10 criteria. These will now have to be updated, and include:

Diagnostic instrument	Abbreviation
Autism Diagnostic Interview (Revised)	ADI.R
Autism Diagnostic Observation Schedule	ADOS
Diagnostic Instrument for Social Communication Disorder	DISCO
Development, Diagnostic and Dimensional Interview	3di

Three of these instruments gather responses given by parents to questions about the child's behaviours at present and in infancy. Diagnosis is, therefore, largely based on parental testimony. Parents are interviewed about:

In the case of ADOS a more objective approach is adopted whereby the child is requested to engage in a number of

Domain	Areas of difficulty:
Social interaction	Eye gaze and facial expressions during interaction Use of body language to both communicate and understand social interactions Ability to develop friendships and peer relationships Ability to empathize and offer comfort to others Ability to share enjoyment with others Giving joint attention during interaction
Social communication	Understanding and using pointing Language development (often delayed or deviant) Using echolalia (echoing words and phrases repeatedly) Using pronominal reversals (confusions with 'I', 'Me', 'You', etc.) Using idiosyncratic speech Using neologisms (inventing words) The quality of the child's conversations including prosody (rhythm and inflection) Literal and metaphorical understanding (e.g. sayings such as 'Keep cool and don't lose your head') Engaging in imaginative and imitative social play Turn-taking in conversation

Restricted and repetitive behaviours	Encompassing preoccupations and circumscribed interests
	Obsessional and solitary activities
	Signs of a rigid adherence to routine or ritual resistance to change
	Stereotyped motor mannerisms such as hand flapping, rocking, spinning objects, tip-toe walking, etc.
	Unusual sensory responses

tasks that demonstrate responses that may be unusual and indicative of ASD. In all cases, however, the responses are coded according to whether the behaviour is normal or abnormal. A score is computed and if the child exceeds the threshold score then a diagnosis of ASD is confirmed.

Although these tests are sophisticated and thoroughly researched, in essence they remain a list of behaviours that the child exhibits. Moreover, since there are multiple items on the list, one child may receive a diagnosis of ASD who exhibits very different patterns of behaviours from that of another child with the same diagnosis. Other developmental disorders occur commonly with ASD, for example, up to 86 per cent of children diagnosed with ASD have verbal learning disorders; more than 50 per cent have Attention Deficit Hyperactivity Disorder (ADHD); and 40 per cent have severe ID. It could be argued that ASD could be viewed in the same way as severe intellectual disabilities, that is, as the common behavioural presentation resulting from a range of different biologically based causes.

In the DSM-5, autism is defined exclusively in terms of behavioural criteria. However, evidence for the biological basis of autism is now well established. There are many investigations demonstrating an association between ASD and genetic and chromosome abnormalities. It is now possible to conduct genetic and chromosome analysis which is more searching and less expensive. But, as yet, these findings are not sufficiently specific or cohesive enough to allow for the identification of clinically meaningful subgroups. It is likely that the future of diagnosis will lie in developments in genetic testing and that ASD will turn out to be a number of distinct genetic disorders with similar behavioural consequences.

It is increasingly recognized that the various types of ASD currently subsumed under the same umbrella may require different educational treatments. There is a need for careful diagnosis over a period of time making use of a battery of tests and procedures in order to determine the appropriate educational programme. This would necessarily involve a longer assessment that could not be completed until the child was at least four or five years of age. It is widely recognized that most parents want answers and advice as early as possible. All parents believe, quite rightly, that the educational intervention should start as soon as possible, but in the rush for early diagnosis there has been a serious danger of over-looking and sacrificing an intensive investigation of the child and of the treatment.

▶ The work of clinicians

It was recommended by the Department for Education and Science (2004) in its 'Good Practice Guidance' that assessment and diagnosis should be carried out by a multi-professional team. Psychologists, speech therapists, psychiatrists, specialist teachers and parents all play an important part in diagnosis. A diagnostic assessment should also review available records and include observation of the child in various settings although both of these are frequently more difficult to arrange. Clinicians who have worked for many years diagnosing and assessing children understand that autism is not one homogeneous disorder with one simple test, so that a great deal rests on their training and professional judgement. There has been a concern that diagnosis has shown geographical variability, some individuals and some centres being more likely to give a positive diagnosis than others. A team approach ensures that conclusions are reached after a due process of discussion and sharing information.

Problems of diagnosis

Children with a diagnosis of ASD resemble one another only insofar as they could be expected to have some difficulties with communication, social interaction and restricted and repetitive behaviours. Research has shown that these behavioural symptoms are relatively independent of one another and it has become evident that there are major differences between children with an ASD diagnosis, not least in terms of the range of intellectual ability. There is concern that this diversity dooms research into a single cause and one specific treatment to ultimate failure. In 2006 Francesca Happé and her associates suggested that attempts to try to identify a single cause to explain ASD should be abandoned.

If a group of children with ASD are being studied and the differences between them in terms of intellect and behaviours are very wide, then any attempt to generalize may be misleading. For example, in a study of a group of children an average IQ score for the group could be derived from individual children with large differences in intelligence. If variation is too wide the relevance of any suggested treatment will be doubtful in many cases. There is a wide disparity in intelligence between those with a diagnosis of ASD. At one extreme, there are those with a diagnosis who are exceptionally bright individuals with university degrees and high-level jobs and there are those who have severe learning difficulties and very low IQs and who require constant care. There are those children with ASD whose expressive language develops relatively normally; there are those children whose language development is severely delayed and remains so. There are children who have delayed language development but who show catch-up effects and there are those children whose language develops normally but their language production fades away. There are children with ASD with evident motor impairments and those children who have no such impairments.

The cognitive ability profiles of children with ASD are varied. Most children with ASD have a discrepancy between their verbal abilities and their performance abilities (but not all). Most have significantly poorer verbal scores and higher scores on visual perceptual tasks, notably on picture puzzle tasks. However, there is a distinct group of children with an ASD diagnosis (between 15 and 20 per cent) who have a cognitive ability profile where verbal abilities are a relative strength and performance skills, including performance on the block design task, are particularly weak (See Chapter 10). This derives from my own data and corresponds with that reported by Patricia Howlin in 2009. Their cognitive profiles are radically different from the majority of autistic subjects.

The standard programmes for the child with ASD now accepted as being the most appropriate, emphasize visual structure and visual learning, particularly the Picture Exchange Communication System (PECS) and Treatment and Education of Autistic and Related Communication Handicapped Children (TEACCH). Using these traditional teaching methods with ASD children who have perceptual difficulties is ineffective. To use pictures or icons with such children merely adds to their frustration. Jigsaws, pictures and visually presented materials are precisely what they cannot understand. These disparities are rarely addressed. Differences in the cognitive profiles of children with ASD are not usually acknowledged as it is mistakenly assumed that they all respond to the same educational interventions. There are distinctly different groups of children who have the same diagnosis but who actually need very different interventions.

For all of these reasons there has been a call for distinguishing subtypes and subgroups which currently exist under the one ASD umbrella. The academic psychologist Ami Klin has suggested that the multiple levels of heterogeneity in ASD are 'One of the greatest obstacles blocking the advancement of research'. Developments in genetic analysis are on the brink of changing the ability of clinicians to investigate differences and establish subtypes of ASD. Significant results about the underlying abnormalities in neurology are also emerging. Improved and more precise diagnosis will lead to more specific treatments and increasingly effective educational interventions.

Diagnosis of ASD without a careful evaluation of the child's cognitive abilities and their strengths and weaknesses can lead to inappropriate treatment and ineffective educational intervention that could add further stress to an already confused and desperate youngster and his or her family. What is apparent in conducting assessments is that children with the same ASD diagnosis can have substantially different cognitive profiles and very rarely does any child meet all the criteria for ASD. Careful and thorough formulation of every child's functioning is needed to inform effective interventions.

Further issues relating to diagnosis

There are a number of other important issues to consider. Although much progress has been made in understanding ASD, some aspects of diagnosis and assessment leave one with some disquiet. Eccentric children with a quirky view of the world and obsessional interests are frequently labelled as having Asperger's syndrome or, as the author recently read, 'atypical mild Asperger's syndrome'. Fitzpatrick said in an article in *The Times* (12.10.09):

> *The tendency to label as autistic every computer geek or eccentric scientist, and every train spotter*

and stamp collector (compounded by the vogue for identifying historical figures and even contemporary celebrities as autistic) carries the danger that the spectrum becomes stretched so wide that autism loses its distinctiveness.

This is a view with which, no doubt, Matthew Parris would concur.

Children as young as 18 months are being diagnosed in the interests of early intervention. Treatment fads come and go. Certain interventions have claimed recovery from autism. Extraordinarily articulate people are writing books or heading conferences explaining what it is like to be autistic. The very fact that these autistic individuals can describe and reflect on their autism is a contra-indication of the condition. It is perhaps unwise to make generalizations from the experiences described by 'high-functioning' people diagnosed with ASD to the experiences of others who may often be unable to speak for themselves. In reality, we cannot know what it is like to be inside the autistic mind. The book *The Reason I Jump* by young Japanese author, Naoki Higashida, claims to provide such an account from the point of view of a severely autistic child but a number of commentators have raised doubts about the validity of such claims. In similar cases Baron-Cohen reminds readers that there have been regular examples of 'facilitated communication' where a zealous caregiver has unintentionally guided the response of the person with ASD who is communicating by pointing to letters or symbols.

It is all a different world from the 1970s when I was engaged in research on autism and clinicians just had Kanner's original conception of autism to consider. Nowadays, psychiatrists and psychologists seem to be under increasing pressure to diagnose ASD from worried parents since they believe that a diagnosis will bring access to better resources. The pressure to diagnose is creating its own momentum. At the same time, parents of children with severe learning difficulties and ASD are becoming increasingly concerned that the public perception of the condition is dominated by that created by articulate and high-functioning individuals who are actually the minority of people with a diagnosis. Their message is that being autistic confers a kind of special status (including the possibility of becoming a member of the 'Aspies' club). The fear is that the needs of those children with severe autism are being neglected or marginalized.

Another concern is that assessment tools are usually behavioural checklists used with parents (with the notable exception of the ADOS). There is no objective, definitive test. Diagnosis relies solely upon behavioural criteria. Parents may not have the necessary developmental perspective and responses are, inevitably, subjective and open to interpretation and bias. Parents of adolescent children are asked questions about their child in infancy relying on their memories when there may be three or four other children in the family. Even in the best available diagnostic questionnaires there is no normative comparison with the general population and little attempt to relate questions to the child's age or cognitive level. Frequently, the IQ level of the subject is ignored. Usually some sort of score is computed and cut-off points or bands of probability of a diagnosis of autism constructed.

The questions are often applied to all children regardless of age or developmental level, and what is abnormal at one age is perfectly normal at another. For example, the obsessive need to line objects up at the age of eight is unusual but it is a regular feature of pre-symbolic play in very young children of average ability.

Similarly, in the most thoroughly researched assessment instruments there is some attempt to weight assessment criteria beyond essential and non-essential, but in many this is not the case. All items are given the same significance in arriving at the cut-off score. Failing to use pointing and gestures is far more significant in terms of diagnosis than tip-toe walking, but both are given the same weighting in many diagnostic checklists. It is possible for a child to get a positive diagnosis on a test because of a large number of minor indicators but have rather few of the essential features. Equally, the best checklists only give cut-off criteria for diagnosis with a simple choice of 'yes' or 'no' as to whether the child shows the specified behaviour.

Labelling: benefits or costs?

It is apparent that the incidence of ASD has been rising. In 2001 in the UK the NAS claimed one in 100 children had ASD. In 2011 this had risen to 1.1 in 100. But is a label of ASD necessarily beneficial to all the children currently being diagnosed? While there are obvious benefits to having a thorough assessment and diagnosis in terms of early intervention and suitable resources, there are also potential costs. There is much psychological and educational research which points out the dangers of labelling children. Expectations and perceptions can actually shape behaviour in children so the label becomes a self-fulfilling prophesy. Therefore, applying any label to a child should never be undertaken lightly. In 2009 a government research project into the prevalence of ASD in the USA found that 40 per cent of children suspected by a health professional of having ASD were not confirmed as such subsequently, and the rate of disconfirmed cases was highest among black children. This suggests that premature labelling of ASD is prevalent. Children's sociability improves with maturity and the label of ASD may be used inappropriately about children from other cultural backgrounds whose mores may be more difficult to comprehend.

Writing in *The Psychologist*, David Pilgrim reviewed the problems of medical labelling and self-fulfilling prophesy effects, and called for a context-specific formulation of mental disorders. He argued that categorical descriptions are 'reductionist, impersonal and stigmatising', and he is critical of what could be regarded as the medicalization of personality. His arguments can be extended to the diagnosis of ASD. We have always had children who were 'loners', 'eccentrics', 'little professors' and 'different'. In other contexts people applaud the lone heroes who blazed trails or held some obsessive conviction against the odds. One problem with the widening definition of ASD is that it takes children who hitherto would have been regarded as eccentric, such as who train spot or keep collections of bugs or like dinosaurs excessively, and turns their behaviour and their interests into 'symptoms'.

A concept of being 'neurotypical' emerged from burgeoning diagnosis. Since people with ASD are assumed to have atypical brain functioning, those without ASD were said to be 'neurotypical' by those with ASD who are articulate and high functioning. This is a somewhat strange state of affairs and a gross over-simplification since in the human gene pool every individual has their own unique range of inherited and mutated genes, and abnormalities. The 'typical' brain is as difficult to find as the 'average' person. Everyone is different, just as no one person with ASD is like another.

Differential diagnosis

ASD is not a single disorder with a single cause. It has been found to exist in association with many genetic and chromosomal disorders. There are a large number of other conditions that occur alongside ASD such as epilepsy and ADHD. This association is known as co-morbidity. Frequently, the child with a diagnosis of ASD will also have another condition and it is now being advocated that a diagnosis of ASD should be regarded as a first step. The clinical psychologist Kenneth Aitken suggests that further genetic investigations should follow.

There are also conditions caused by environmental factors which appear to mirror ASD. One of these is Reactive Attachment Disorder (RAD). RAD has come to prominence as part of the growing awareness and understanding of Attachment Theory. Infants with RAD present with either clinging behaviour or physical withdrawal. They give limited eye contact, have minimal interest in toys or in other children and can have self-soothing behaviours such as rocking and hand wringing. Speech and language development are often delayed. Their approach to other people may be marked by anxiety or by indiscriminate attention seeking. One can see why an initial appraisal of such symptoms might lead to a suggestion of ASD as the diagnosis. There is the risk that autism and RAD can be confounded given the similarity of symptoms.

The essential feature of RAD is that the severely disturbed social behaviour results from early experiences of negative and inappropriate care-giving involving the persistent disregard of the child's basic needs. Neglect rather than a neurological impairment is the causal issue. Children with ASD do not have a history of neglect and typically show restricted, repetitive behaviours not evident in children with RAD. Clinicians involved in assessment and differential diagnosis of the two conditions are advised that the possibility of ASD should be eliminated first.

Some concerns have been raised in recent years about the possibility that ASD is a social construction describing a range of children whose behaviour we find to be difficult and challenging. In a book published in 2010 entitled *The Myth of Autism*, the authors make some cogent arguments. They point out that there are huge cultural differences in the behaviours linked to diagnosis. Children with ASD frequently fail to use gestures and this is a diagnostic marker, but the use of gestures is actively discouraged and considered impolite in some cultures. Of course, the notion that ASD is merely a social construction is both distressing and confusing for hard-pressed parents who have found the assessment and diagnosis of their child has been hard-won but helpful.

Introduction to interventions and treatment in ASD (Levels 1–3)

The range of difficulties that can lead to a diagnosis of ASD means that you can be tall, medium or short; slight, average or heavily built; have a large head, a regular sized head or a small head; be learning disabled, of normal IQ or of high intelligence. You may or may not have epilepsy; you may or may not have gastrointestinal problems...

you might or might not benefit from any of a range of specific treatments, supplements, therapies or other interventions.

ALL THAT MATTERS

Kenneth Aitken

▶ Background

Despite the fact that there are similarities in the behaviours they present, no one treatment or intervention can suit all those with ASD. Those working with children with ASD need to provide an individualized intervention programme which will be different in every case. The following interventions which have been used by the author over many years with many children are all evidence based, but must be seen as a 'pick and mix' approach. Some will work and some will be inappropriate. As Rita Jordan, an expert in the education of children with ASD, has pointed out, in devising any intervention it is essential to know the child with ASD very well first.

A debate has been ongoing among educators who have endeavoured to help those with a diagnosis of ASD to learn efficiently. The question is, should programmes seek to address the inherent weaknesses in the hope that deficits can show improvement? An alternative approach seeks to build on the evident strengths in order to develop self-confidence and encourage greater incidental learning. An example of the latter approach is the Kaufman's Son-Rise system where the children with ASD are allowed to choose their own interests and thereby lead their own educational programme.

Level 3 in DSM-5 describes children with severe autism. They are those requiring 'very substantial support'. Most children with severe autism also have significant learning difficulties and will attend a special school. Within the classroom, such children find it difficult to:

- Comprehend instructions and social interactions

- Cope with change in routines

- Recognize beginnings and endings

- Understand the passage of time

- Organize themselves, their time, their tasks and their belongings

- Master the individual skills contained within parts of a sequence and then sequence those skills

Children with 'Level 2 Needs' may attend an ordinary school which has specialist provision such as a special unit offering small group provision. Children at Level 1 can usually cope with ordinary school and the ordinary class but they need assistance within the classroom and playground. In all cases parents should be heavily involved in the educational programme for their child because every child is different. Parents have a great deal to contribute to an understanding and management of their child. They will also seek to promote the best outcomes.

In the following chapters interventions at the three levels of severity are outlined but some general principles are covered first. The standard programmes for the child with ASD at all levels of severity, now accepted as being the most appropriate, emphasize routine, visual structure, visual learning and social and communication skills. The most frequently used interventions are:

- The PECS
- TEACCH

▶ Behaviour modification approaches such as Applied Behavioural Analysis (ABA). NB: this is not specific to ASD

▶ A number of language programmes such as Social Use of Language designed to improve social comprehension and interaction

All programmes for children with ASD emphasize the following:

1 Routine and structure

Children with ASD thrive on routine. The key to understanding the importance of this lies in appreciating the difficulties people with ASD are likely to have in trying to make sense of their environment. Change creates stress. While routine is crucial, it is also important to be aware that children with ASD are likely to become heavily dependent on their routines and the predictability it affords. As the child's confidence grows, a routine should be deliberately varied, in detail rather than in essentials, to reflect reality, and to encourage greater flexibility. Changes are, nevertheless, likely to cause upset. The young person, therefore, needs to be notified and given an explanation for any change in advance.

2 Use of timetables

A variety of strategies can be employed to help the child with ASD to become better orientated, better organized and more secure. These include the use of maps, personal storage space, home-school book, personalized timetables and schedules. When designing a personalized timetable for someone with ASD, there are a number of important points to consider, such as accessibility, visual appeal, recreational time and lists of belongings. Again, the aim is to provide structure while encouraging flexibility.

3 Classroom organization

Many pupils and students with ASD respond best in a rather formal learning setting, where there is limited free movement around the room. Adaptations to the room may include:

▶ Well-defined personal work space in a quiet corner of the room where others will not be passing by frequently

▶ Removal of distracting materials from near the work space

People with ASD prefer a clearly defined, predictable routine to the day. This means that there needs to be careful preparation for when changes of routines are planned, such as school visits, trips, or extracurricular activities.

4 Visual presentations

Children with ASD usually learn best through visual input. Language is usually a relative weakness. Visual prompts may help to promote confidence, such as a sequence of activity cards for each day and a visual timetable for the weekly cycle.

5 Addressing sensory difficulties

Those working with children with ASD need to be aware that such children often experience heightened or diminished reactions to noise, touch and pain. Trigger points can cause stress, for example, particular loud noises, such as tables and chairs being moved, large, open, echoing spaces, such as the dining hall or gymnasium can all be very aversive and cause distressed reactions.

6 Understanding the pupil with ASD

Every child with ASD presents with different facets of the condition and varies in cognitive ability. It is imperative that those working with the child have an understanding both of autism but also the strengths, weaknesses, likes and dislikes of the child. Each individual may have very personal stress triggers which can cause fear and/or anger. Understanding these ensures the child is in a position to learn efficiently.

▶ Level 3 interventions

The majority of children with severe ASD also have severe learning difficulties. Level 3 interventions will address both factors. Targets are likely to include:

1 Object reference and cause and effect

2 Establishing joint attention

3 Establishing communication

4 Visual learning and structure (TEACCH)

5 Building communication and reducing repetitive and isolated behaviours

6 Preparing for change

7 Remembering

Children at the more able end of the autistic continuum (IQ above 85) will vary considerably according to the degree to which they are affected by autism. High intelligence enables children with ASD to overcome their impairments more easily. They can learn and apply strategies more efficiently. However, there are some very able individuals who are severely afflicted with autism. These are the people who may, for example, have high-level academic qualifications, perhaps a PhD in Physics, but who never marry, have a limited social life, and who need support for all the complexities of the social aspects of day-to-day living. Most of the more able children with ASD, however, can learn strategies for contending with social life and they are able to go to an ordinary school. Some can cope with the demands of further and higher education. They will require varying degrees of support within the school, college or university. However, some may be more appropriately placed in a special unit or a language unit or some similar special educational provision. These children can initially appear to be sociable and articulate, although they often have difficulties in dealing with complex aspects of life in a community.

▶ Level 2 interventions

These usually take the form of target work in relation to:

General	Specific
SOCIAL COMMUNICATION	Interacting and making sense of people Understanding and listening Conversations Moderating communication
REPETITION AND RIGIDITY	Preparing for change
SENSORY MOTOR DIFFICULTIES	Inappropriate reactions to sound, touch and visual stimuli
EMOTIONAL DIFFICULTIES	Encouraging motivation and limiting over-dependency

▶ Level 1 interventions

Interventions at the least severe level may include many of the targets listed at Level 2 and additionally:

SOCIAL COMMUNICATION	Friendships Residual language difficulties
RIGIDITY	Coping with the unexpected
EMOTIONAL REGULATION	Managing self-control and anger Anxiety and depression
WORK SKILLS	Personal organization Classroom skills

Interventions in ASD (Level 3 – Severe)

ALL THAT MATTERS

The DSM-5 describes the severity levels for ASD Level 3, as:

▶ Requiring very substantial support

▶ Severe deficits in verbal and non-verbal social communication skills

▶ Severe impairments in functioning

▶ Very limited initiation of social interactions and minimal response to social overtures from others

▶ Inflexibility of behaviour

▶ Extreme difficulty coping with change

▶ Restricted/repetitive behaviours which markedly interfere with functioning in all spheres

▶ Great distress/difficulty changing focus or action.

▶ Introduction

Children with severe autism frequently have substantial intellectual impairments. The absence of or significant delays in language development necessarily impede thinking, logical deduction and reasoning since these are arguably dependent on internal language. I know of no case of a child with severe ASD without speech who has been assessed as 'high functioning'. In this section there is consideration of those 40 per cent of children with a diagnosis of ASD who also have severe ID.

In 2010 MENCAP, in collaboration with the UK Department of Health, produced guidelines for improving socialization and communication in children with severe learning disabilities entitled, 'What Works and Why this is Essential'. It was pointed out that people with ASD may be capable of good concentration but what they choose to concentrate on can be very idiosyncratic. Youngsters with ASD may have difficulty picking out what they should focus on, especially if they haven't listened to, or understood, the instructions. They may be particularly vulnerable to distractions from external sources and seem to have difficulty in filtering out irrelevant stimuli (particularly sounds and visual information). If they are finding the environment stressful, children with ASD may actively withdraw into their own fantasy world or into their restricted obsessions.

A fundamental strategy for many youngsters with severe ASD, therefore, is to provide high levels of structure. This works at a number of different levels. If practical, it can be extremely helpful to establish a separate work station where independent work is to be completed. Ideally this needs to offer as few distractions as possible, away from busy areas, facing a blank wall and possibly screened in some way. It is necessary to make sure all work materials are available and organized before the session starts. The aim is to build an association between this location and getting work done.

The report described current interventions in detail. It identified the following important principles:

▪ Taking time to become familiar with the child's personality and communication style

▪ Constancy of approach using familiar, predictable routines

▪ Talking in short simple phrases to facilitate personal understanding

- Using music and giving opportunities to make choices

- Causing interactions and encouraging reciprocal responding

▶ Targets for intervention for parents, teachers, assistants or other carers

1 Object reference and cause and effect

New-born children are faced with what William James described as a 'blooming buzzing confusion'. A world of light, sight, sound, touch, smell and taste assails the child. Gradually, the child recognizes certain objects and events; faces, toys, noises, all reoccur and become familiar. One of the primary cognitive developments is recognition of objects and their permanence in the environment even when they are out of sight. They have not ceased to exist and the infant anticipates their return. Similarly, another important discovery occurring in the first months after birth is that of cause and effect. The infant accidently hits a mobile toy and a tune starts to play. The movement is repeated and achieves the same result. Children with profound ASD and ID can be extremely delayed in these two important aspects of cognition.

Strategies for intervention

(i) **Cause and effect activities.** This approach has been used with people with profound ID who lack understanding that their actions have consequences and they can make things happen. People with profound impairment can use micro switches or touch screens to convey choices and attract the attention of others. An application has been the development of a system known as 'Big Mac' which is a single message communication device. A message can be recorded on it and played when a switch is pressed.

(ii) **Objects of reference.** This is a method that allows the child with severe autism to use objects as a concrete link between language and the environment. Objects of reference can be used to signal what is about to happen, such as lunchtime, for example, or to offer choices. Objects become symbols of predictable events and can be seen as a precursor to language.

2 Establishing joint attention

Babies are highly responsive to their primary care-giver, usually the mother, and from their earliest days mother and baby attune to one another in what is described as 'sensitive intersubjectivity'. This is the ability to build a close, trusting bond where meaning is shared. This attachment lays the foundation for communication and mothers of children with severe autism often report that their child was unusually 'good' and 'placid', 'rarely cried', but was 'floppy and unresponsive'. Babies need to learn to look at their mothers, to look where she is looking and to respond to her interaction and to share her gaze.

Strategies for intervention

(i) **Intensive interaction.** This approach is based on the work of Dave Hewett and Melanie Nind and focuses on developing interaction and communication between people with complex communication needs and those around them. It uses the highly responsive individualized interactions between babies and primary care-givers.

3 Establishing communication

Teachers who have worked for years with children with severe ASD and ID will frequently report that the real breakthrough occurs when the child brings them an object, points at something or verbalizes meaningfully with a single word. It can take many months for this to occur but it is the start of communication. Signing systems can be developed and exchanging pictures or icons for responses are both the precursors to verbal communication and the development of a basic vocabulary.

Strategies for intervention

(i) Non-verbal: PECS. This approach emphasizes the transactional nature of communication for children with ASD. They are taught to exchange a picture or symbol of an object which they currently desire and to bring that picture to the parent, teacher or key worker who will then satisfy that need. A vocabulary of pictures is created and this can include actions as well as objects. Another promising development is PROLOQUO2GO which involves a systematic symbol system using icons and an iPad.

(ii) Signing, including Makaton and Signalong.

Although people with severe ASD frequently have difficulty in using and interpreting gestures and facial expression, Makaton, Signalong and British Sign Language have been used routinely with such children in order to facilitate and enhance attempts at communication. The use of Makaton with children with ASD has been evaluated and shown to be effective in improving communication. Other researchers have pointed out that for signing systems to be systematic and effective then all staff should use the method automatically. They suggest that embedding a signing culture in the school or home is most successful way of developing communication.

(iii) **Verbal: Augmented and Alternative Communication (AAC) including voice output communication aids.** AACs range from single method devices like the Big Mac System to complex and highly flexible voice output aids. Between these two extremes are a number of electronic devices that can be used to communicate a small range of pre-determined messages. For example, in the Step-by-Step Communicator a series of pre-recorded messages can be played back by successive presses on switches. There is now an extensive body of research showing effectiveness of hi-tech AAC especially for those with ASD who have a natural liking for technical equipment.

(iv) **Music therapy and other arts-based approaches.** Music therapy and using music to aid communication to soothe children with ASD is a well-established therapeutic approach. It may be particularly helpful in establishing turn-taking. Art therapy is also widely favoured since it taps into the visual and perceptual strengths of children with ASD.

4 Visual learning and structure (TEACCH)

One of the best approaches to teaching children with severe autism is the TEACCH system devised by Mesibov and Schopler in North Carolina, USA and used throughout the world.

Strategies for intervention

(i) **The use of visual timetables, symbols and pictures.** One of the key features of TEACCH was the realization that children with ASD often have reasonably well-developed visual and perceptual abilities but profound social and language difficulties.

Communication that employed symbols and pictures was found to be more effective than verbal communication. They can be used both receptively and expressively, to help someone:

▶ Understand what is about to happen or what choices are available

▶ Request things

▶ Make comments about the environment

Visual timetables and visual instructions are now commonplace and a communication board is often used where symbols can be displayed.

(ii) **Visual prompts** can be very helpful:

▶ They can be used to show the pupil what activities are coming next (particularly useful if they are motivating to the child)

▶ At a more detailed level they can show the steps in the particular task

▶ Symbols or words can also be used to remind the pupil of basic rules and expectations

External time limits (using a kitchen timer or similar) combined with very specific work assignments may help the child focus. If this can also be linked to incentives this may motivate the child with autism to make the effort needed to resist distractions.

(iii) **Tasks need to be very carefully and clearly structured.**

▶ The steps need to be spelled out explicitly and the expected end product described in concrete detail.

▶ It is important to be realistic about the pace of work and level of concentration expected. If the child is receiving one-to-one help this can be quite intense and demanding.

The child may not be able to keep up this pace through the whole day and will need regular breaks.

(iv) **Use of the 'Buddy System'.** Depending on relationships with classmates, it can be useful to use a good friend or 'Buddy System', with other children offering occasional reminders to concentrate (using some agreed prompt or code word).

5 Building communication and reducing repetitive and isolated behaviours

There are several approaches to helping the child with severe ASD enter regular social communication with others. This often leads to a diminution of their isolated, ritualistic and repetitive behaviours. The child psychologist Elizabeth Newson suggested that obsessive behaviours such as ordering, counting, spinning, etc., could become a means of interacting with the child by turning these rituals into games and engaging in the child's world.

Strategies for intervention

(i) **Story and narrative approaches.** This is a growing area in research and practice with a diversity of methods which share a common theme. The schemes use a combination of language, pictures and multi-sensory props to construct a simple narrative. The aim is to aid the understanding of the social dimension in personal situations and events.

(ii) **Social stories.** Carol Gray (teacher and expert in ASD) details the effects of writing an individualized story which describes a specific social situation in terms of the relevant social cues and responses. She provides guidance about the relative proportions of descriptive (as opposed to prescriptive) sentences to be used and recommends mentioning other people's perspectives as well.

(iii) **Pictures of me.** This is a very specific example of the 'Social Story' method. With the support of a trusted adult, the youngster is involved in collaboratively writing and illustrating a booklet about him or herself. Through a carefully thought-out sequence the young person is helped to understand their own personality and talents. After this, they can focus on the difficulties and needs which arise as a result of ASD. An outline of the approach is provided by Carol Gray.

(iv) **Social use of language programme.** This approach was developed by Wendy Rinaldi and is aimed at enhancing the social communication of children of primary age but is especially suitable for older children with ASD and severe learning difficulties. It also includes teaching activities for specific interactive skills (including awareness of self and others) and suggestions for practising skills in social contexts.

(v) **Social skills training with children and adolescents.** This is a comprehensive programme developed by Sue Spence covering most areas of social behaviour. It was originally devised for socially inept youngsters rather than for children with ASD but has proved very valuable for work with them. The programme covers understanding and using body language, gestures, facial expressions and eye contact as well as using direct conversation. Details of this approach are given in her book.

(vi) **Mindreading and the Transporters DVD.** Simon Baron-Cohen and his associates have developed software to teach emotional recognition to children with ASD. The Transporters DVD animates Thomas the Tank Engine characters to demonstrate emotions, building on one of the regular obsessions of boys with ASD.

6 Preparing for change

All children with severe ASD need structure and routines. They enjoy repetition and rituals. They can spend hours on seemingly pointless tasks, shredding paper, dividing blades of grass, spinning objects, rocking rhythmically and so on. Changes to routines or intrusions into their rituals can cause major problems, temper tantrums and sometimes self-harming. The child is evidently very upset. The world must be a frightening place and having routines ensures sameness and familiarity. They may be frightened by the uncertainty of not being able to predict what comes next. The child may be happily obsessed with one repetitive activity but the aim is to shape the behaviour into activities that allow for improved communication and co-operation.

Strategies for intervention

(i) Go along with the child's need for routines. Build a timetable which clearly shows the regular pattern. For example:

- Choose a particular word, picture, line drawing or symbol to go with each part of the daily routine. Mount these on separate cards which can be put in a photograph album

- Get the child into the habit of taking out the card at the start of the activity and putting it away at the end. The link between a particular card and the activity it stands for needs to be understood

(ii) Once the link between the cards and the activities is understood, start to arrange the pictures to show the order of the routine for the next half day. It may be feasible to build up to a whole day.

(iii) Before starting an activity, the person with ASD can be instructed to 'go and get the card'. This will explain what will happen next.

- Once the person is used to the timetable, it may be possible to introduce one or two changes of activity.

- These can be pointed out well ahead of them happening.

- The fact that the person gets advance warning of what is going to happen and what will follow will help them cope with change.

(iv) Some changes may be difficult for the person to understand in advance, particularly if it involves a new place or new people. Video recordings or photographs can be used to prepare for this.

(v) It may be helpful for the person to take something that is familiar into the new situation, in the same way that very young children use a cuddly blanket or a soft toy.

(vi) It is important to use very simple, precise language that will explain what is happening.

7 Remembering

Most people with severe ASD have difficulty accessing information from their memory. Often they seem to need a very precise and specific cue. They need to be taught sequences in small steps which need to be repeated regularly. Many have difficulty responding to open questions, for example, 'What did you do at school today?' but are able to answer questions with forced alternatives, e.g., 'Did you go horse riding or swimming today?'

Strategies for intervention

(i) Use 'backward chaining' to teach life skills. This entails breaking down the steps of a task and teaching them in reverse order with the last step in the sequence first. This is exemplified in teaching a child to dress.

(ii) Provide the child with cues which help in the retrieval of information from memory. Key words or PECS can serve as reminders to trigger the child's memory.

(iii) Communication between home and school via a home-school book is important.

(iv) Open questions are difficult and you should only use these when the child can retrieve the answer from his or her memory. Asking questions which will serve as a cue, such as forced alternatives, is a better approach.

(v) If the child is expected to memorize specific information encourage active rehearsal. There are a number of helpful techniques, such as trying to build the information into a diagram or picture and helping the person to build personal links between new information or concepts and what is already known.

(vi) Use mnemonics, encourage rehearsal and make use of web diagrams, photographs and drawings.

(vii) When talking about experiences with the child emphasize any personal involvement and reactions to the activities which will facilitate recall.

Interventions in ASD (Level 2)

The DSM-5 describes the severity levels for ASD Level 2 as:

▶ Requiring substantial support

▶ Marked deficits in verbal and non-verbal social communication skills

▶ Social impairments apparent even with supports in place

▶ Limited initiation of social interactions and reduced or abnormal responses to social overtures from others

▶ Inflexibility of behaviour

▶ Difficulty coping with change

▶ Restricted/repetitive behaviours which appear frequently enough to be obvious to the casual observer and interfere with functioning in a variety of contexts

▶ Distress and/or difficulty changing focus or action

1 Interacting and making sense of people

When we talk to someone we use a range of non-verbal signals, such as facial expression, body language and eye contact to help to get our message across. People with ASD have trouble working out the meaning of these signals. Some may find it easier to listen and understand if they block out the non-verbal signals (for example, by not looking at the speaker). Some may experience great difficulty in 'putting themselves in other people's shoes'. It might be very hard for them to grasp what another person is thinking or feeling. They may not understand why a person might be saying something just for fun. The person with ASD may have great difficulty in coping with the double meanings that are essential parts of humour.

Young people with ASD often feel lost or confused. This may lead them to opt out and follow their own idiosyncratic behaviours. Some children may have difficulty making sense of the unwritten and flexible rules that govern playground activities. They also have problems in understanding the 'rules' about how people relate to each other. Even in one-to-one situations some find the demands of relating to other people too difficult to deal with and will seek to avoid or minimize contact. Where such contact cannot be avoided they may try to control the interaction by sticking to specific topics of conversation. Work in less structured group situations or simply having to sit close to a large group can be an anxious experience. Unfortunately, people with ASD are particularly vulnerable to teasing and unkind behaviour.

How to help

(i) The raised voice, animated expressions and forceful gestures which we tend to use instinctively can get in the way of comprehension. All this extra information can be distracting. Speak as calmly and clearly as possible if there have been problems.

(ii) Make a point of showing the child with ASD appropriate gestures in a natural setting. For example, thumbs up, nodding assent, shaking head for 'No'. If the child uses excessive gesture use simple strategies to help. For example, getting the child to keep their hands in their pockets or to hold something to reduce flapping.

(iii) The person with ASD often cannot read between the lines. It may be necessary to explain exactly what is meant particularly when it involves behaviour in social situations.

(iv) The person in charge may need to explain how to tell if someone is joking (as opposed to bullying); how another person might be feeling and how to tell if someone has done something 'on purpose' (rather than by accident). The person with ASD will probably always have to work out these sorts of things logically or 'by the rules' rather than sensing them intuitively.

(v) The child may be helped by games and role play activities which involve thinking about another person's viewpoint.

(vi) It may be necessary to teach particular behaviours to deal with specific situations, for example, how to behave when someone is cross, trying to be helpful or wanting to play. The person with ASD may always find it difficult to respond intuitively or naturally, but can be taught what to do to prevent things from being made worse. The aim is to provide a simple 'script' or guidelines.

(vii) If it is felt that free time is too confusing or upsetting it may be best to find ways of providing more structured activities.

(viii) In a school situation building support among their peers is useful. The 'Circle of Friends' technique uses a group of friends in practical problem solving and as a source of emotional support for the person with ASD.

(ix) The child with ASD may need to be 'de-sensitized' to group activities. This involves gradually encouraging participation in activities which entail involvement in higher levels of contact. To begin with, the emphasis may need to be only on tolerating physical proximity. Some youngsters do not want to make friends or spend all their time in other people's company. This needs to be respected. As with any child, there should be room for free play even if it is rather autistic. Thought should be given to having a private place for time out.

2 Understanding and listening

It is very common for people with ASD to interpret what other people say and mean in a very literal, concrete way. Figures of speech (such as, 'stretch your legs'; 'have a short break'; 'face the music'), humour and sarcasm may pose particular problems. In schools it is very common to use indirect (and polite) forms of speech such as, 'Can you put your books away?' or 'Would you like to sit down?' These are actually instructions but may be treated as questions by the person with ASD. Part of this difficulty is caused by the problems in interpreting the speaker's intentions and motivation. This requires making sense of non-verbal clues and, in part, on being able to put oneself in the speaker's shoes. Some people with ASD cannot take in group instructions, perhaps not understanding that they are one of the group and that the instruction is meant for them as well as for the other people. Some have found ways of appearing to listen while actually not attending. This skill avoids them being singled out. Some people with ASD develop alternative coping strategies when unable to follow group instructions. A common one is to copy what the other children do. This may mask serious comprehension problems.

How to help

(i) It would be impossible to stop using all metaphors and figures of speech. However, it is possible to check back on what has been said and rephrase the comment if necessary. For example, rather than, 'Please give me a hand' one might say 'Please help me'. Explain some common idioms, metaphors and sayings, such as 'too many cooks'; 'making hay'; 'burying his head'; 'turning a blind eye'.

(ii) Use simple, short and direct sentences, putting emphasis on what is required rather than on what is not. So that one might say 'Please be quiet!' as opposed to 'I don't want all this noise, thank you'. Beware of double negatives.

(iii) Children with ASD can be encouraged to monitor their own understanding and given support as to what to do if they don't understand.

(iv) A child with ASD may enjoy humour at a basic level. For example, visual slapstick humour or knock-knock jokes. However, it may be necessary to discourage the child from using these inappropriately or 'going over the top'.

(v) Pupils with ASD often need to have instructions repeated, especially when the teacher has been addressing a group. It may be sufficient to mention the child's name so that the child knows of their inclusion in the group.

3 Conversations

People with ASD can have serious difficulty in knowing how and when to join conversations. They may not recognize the pauses and subtle signals which invite them to join in the conversation. They may appear to be rude and boorish. They may lack the skills of commenting or building on the contribution of another speaker. They may become so pre-occupied with a particular thought or topic that they cannot resist blurting it out. Children with ASD may learn their language skills by copying 'chunks' of language which they hear. This will include not just the adult's language but also their intonation. Many people with ASD lack an intuitive understanding of social rules and expectations in these situations.

How to help

(i) In group situations an object such as a stone or bean bag can be used with everyone understanding that only the person holding it is allowed to speak ('Circle Time' technique).

(ii) The child will need opportunities to observe how peers speak and interact with others. It may be necessary to teach that pauses in conversation are the places to come in with comments. The child may need to practise recognizing pauses and 'reading' eye signals. In this way they can come to understand that when someone gives direct eye contact and pauses, they may be indicating that 'it's your turn' to speak, whereas averted eye gaze means 'it's my turn'. Watching and discussing DVDs or television programmes might be useful in interpreting patterns of interaction.

(iii) If the child continues to have serious difficulty in recognizing when and how to join in, then it may be necessary to devise an agreed signal, (e.g. hand gesture, holding up an object) to be used by supportive adults or peers. It may be necessary for the child with ASD to rehearse these techniques.

4 Moderating communication

A common feature of people with ASD is the tendency to talk about an obsessional interest to the exclusion of other topics and without regard to the listener's interests. This sort of obsession may serve the function of reducing anxiety just as other forms of ritual do. Alternatively, people with ASD may be doing this because they actually want to engage in conversation, but don't know the conventions of how to 'chat'. Some youngsters with ASD are extremely rigid in their conversations and enjoy hearing the same answer over and over again, for example, 'When is it lunchtime?' expecting the response, 'At one o'clock', and being extremely upset if an alternative answer is given such as, 'Soon'. The child with ASD lacks flexibility in conversation.

How to help

(i) Respect all attempts at communication and give the child time to ask questions when appropriate. This may act as a 'calming' strategy and allow time to engage in more purposeful communication later. Obsessive talking may be a way of covering anxiety, in which case it will be important to keep the child calm and give reassurance.

(ii) The child could use appropriate calming strategies, for example, listening to music on a headset, reading a favourite book, having a favoured toy.

(iii) It is important to understand the reasons why the child obsesses about a topic and to reduce the extent to which it is allowed to intrude on his or her thoughts and conversations. Identify 'special times' when the child can talk about interests and actively discourage these topics at all other times. Gradually, the duration and number of these special times can be reduced.

(iv) The opportunity to talk about the child's obsessional subjects can also be used as a reward. Alternatively, when the child is not talking about an obsessional interest, it should be noted and the child praised.

(v) Use the child's interests in talking about favourite topics as a way of developing conversational knowledge.

(vi) Teach when and with whom it is appropriate to talk about obsessions. Explicit directions will be required for this to be achieved.

(vii) If the obsession is socially appropriate look for opportunities to promote the child's interests with peers. They may often show great expertise on their subject of interest, such as makes of car, types of trains, weather patterns, models of washing machine.

(viii) Use the child's repetitive questioning as a learning opportunity. Tell the child that questions will be answered when your requests have been complied with. Gradually ration the time for responding to repetitive questioning, for example, 'I can't answer you now, but I can talk to you at 11 o'clock for five minutes'. It is important to ensure that this is what duly occurs.

(ix) Be explicit in limiting the questioning but invite more appropriate conversation, 'This question is boring, but ask me something else' (or 'talk to me about...').

5 Preparing for change

Children with ASD need a sense of order and stability. If established expectations change or appear fluid they may become anxious. Explicit expectations provide useful boundaries for people with ASD. For example, always say 'Hello' and 'Goodbye'; 'brush your teeth every morning and evening'. But due to a difficulty with flexible thought, they may not appreciate that there are times and situations where routines can be renegotiated or changed. Some may be unable to appreciate why a person might not have strictly adhered to a rule.

People with ASD may have difficulty predicting future events. Because of this, some insist on things happening in a set order. This order provides a sense of security and comfort. They can also have a strong need to complete something once they have started it. This compulsion can take priority over whatever else they should be doing and they may become very upset if unable to finish. They often make rigid connections, frequently based on a single experience. Some aspect of such a situation may have caused them distress in the past; similar situations then trigger exactly the same reactions. The fear may also attach to other, quite different situations.

How to help

(i) It is important to start, wherever possible, by finding out what it is that the child dislikes. This is best achieved by asking the child directly. Most people with ASD can tell us about their fears, but we often forget to ask them. Once their fear is understood then realistic targets can be set and coping mechanisms established.

(ii) The child is likely to adhere strictly to any rule. It is therefore important to think carefully about how the rules are worded, building some flexibility into them.

(iii) Because the child will have difficulty understanding why rules are not always strictly adhered to, make sure someone explains changes to the child, preferably giving good warning. For example, 'Tomorrow we are not going to see Aunty Jean because she's on holiday'.

(iv) Social stories will help to explain why people sometimes bend or break rules.

(v) The length of time it takes to get through a routine can gradually be reduced beginning with one step at a time. A kitchen timer can be useful as a visual prompt.

(vi) When the child becomes comfortable with reductions in times for routines, introduce a timetable. This provides structure and reassurance.

6 Sensory difficulties: inappropriate reactions to sound, touch and visual stimuli

Unusual reactions or over-sensitivity to specific noises are quite common in people with ASD. Some may be irritated and distracted by noises occurring in the environment, such as the lawn being mowed, an aeroplane passing overhead, or a lorry on the road. Some may place their hands over their ears or make humming noises. Some will be distractible and find it difficult to pay attention when the noises which distress them are nearby. They may actually find noise painful or intrusive.

People with ASD often display a heightened, over-exaggerated response to touch. When touched by another person in an unpredictable way the individual may show a 'flight' or 'fight' response. Alternatively, they may touch people inappropriately, for example, having a fascination with blonde hair. People with ASD may like the person who has hugged them, but not like the sudden physical contact. Some like physical contact if it is on their terms. It can also be difficult for a youngster with ASD to make sense of what the touch is intended to mean. The child may not recognize that the other person is trying to be friendly or just attracting attention.

Some people with ASD may stare through people and avoid looking them in the eye. They may appear clumsy and ungainly, often seeming hesitant about negotiating steps and kerbs or other obstacles. They often pay no attention to peers but will locate a tiny scrap of paper on the floor and give it most careful and prolonged inspection. They may find it hard to determine which piece of visual information is relevant, and rarely see the bigger picture. Some might be unable to tolerate bright, flickering lights or sunlight and may be considerably calmer when in a darkened room. Certain light can even be painful. Others have a particular fascination for light, especially twinkling light.

How to help

(i)   Cut down as many sources of extraneous noise as possible, or be aware of triggers likely to cause a reaction.

(ii) There are always going to be certain sounds and noises in the environment which may upset the child with ASD. It will be necessary gradually to expose them to these stimuli to increase their tolerance and ability to cope appropriately when they occur.

(iii) Problems of sensitivity to noise can also be tackled using social stories which explain that they occur naturally.

(iv) If the child is sensitive to touch approach the child from the front and give a clear verbal explanation of what is going to happen. It is important that everyone in contact with the child is aware of the sensitivity.

(v)   If the child has become distressed always de-brief the child after an incident. Use simple, clear language. Explain why the situation occurred and discuss what the child could have done, maybe modelling a more appropriate reaction.

(vi) Teach some calming strategies to help the child cope with an incident. These could be some relaxation/breathing exercises or the use of a mantra such as, 'stay calm'.

(vii) Children with ASD work best in a distraction-free work area. This might mean turning the child's desk so that it faces a blank wall to limit visual stimuli. Limit the visual distraction in the environment by making it as structured as possible. Work areas, worksheets, even display spaces, where possible, should not involve 'cluttered' visual information.

(viii) If the child has difficulty giving eye contact, respect this. However, the child can be taught socially acceptable ways of giving minimal eye contact by occasional glances and smiles.

7 Encouraging motivation and limiting over-dependence

The social sources of motivation that work with many youngsters don't seem to operate as strongly with children with ASD. They may not be as interested in pleasing people or modelling themselves on a favourite adult. Limitations of imagination may make long-term incentives such as good exam results, good career prospects, marriage and adult responsibilities ineffective. Adolescents with ASD may be so preoccupied with their emotional difficulties that they have little energy to focus on school work.

Many children with ASD get locked into patterns of doing things in the same way and with the same people. They become fixed into routines of high dependency. Some children do not have the social motivation to be independent. Equally, the supporting adult needs to allow the child to do some things independently.

How to help

(i) As soon as the child has learned a few skills set up a time each day when these can be practised independently, ensuring that the tasks are well within capabilities. The focus should be on developing independence as well as on the specific task.

(ii) It is always worth trying to use any obsessive interest as a source of reward and motivation; for example, 'if you complete this work by 10.30, then you get 10 minutes on your dinosaur project'.

(iii) To help understanding of what is expected, make independent work as structured as possible; for example, sitting at a special table, with tasks sequenced and clear indicators of when to start and finish. Expectations about quantity and quality of work output need to be explicit and detailed. It is better to use very short-term targets to begin with, gradually extending their duration

(iv) Praise the child every time tasks are successfully completed unsupported. It is important for the child to know when work time and the task are finished. For example, this could be indicated verbally or with a 'finished' card. The TEACCH project uses a 'Finished Basket'. External incentives of some kind are likely to be helpful. However, it is better to reward 'little and often'. It is always better to ask the child for ideas about possible rewards/incentives.

Some children with Level 2 severity will also benefit from the interventions described for Level 1 especially later in life as more skills are acquired.

Interventions in ASD (Level 1 – Mild)

ALL THAT
MATTERS

The DSM-5 describes the severity levels for ASD Level 1 as:

▶ Without supports in place, deficits in social communication cause noticeable impairments

▶ Difficulty initiating social interactions

▶ Atypical or unsuccessful responses to the social overtures of others and apparent decreased interest in social interactions

▶ Inflexibility of behaviour which causes significant interference with functioning in one or more contexts

▶ Difficulty switching between activities

▶ Problems of organisation and planning hamper independence

It is important to note that the DSM-5 indicates that following the reorganization of diagnostic assessments, those who might previously have been described as having Asperger's Disorder (they would mainly have fallen into Level I) should in future be given the diagnosis of ASD.

1 Friendships

People with mild ASD often want the friendship of others but do not understand the subtle complexities of making and keeping friends. It can be very difficult for some to pick up the social cues that invite social interaction. When trying to make conversation the person with ASD may not read the non-verbal signals which are involved in turn-taking. They may not appreciate the clues which the listener is giving about the relevance and interest of the chosen topic. The person with ASD may talk at the listener endlessly and in excessive detail about obscure subjects that are of special interest to them. Some people with ASD may stand too close, use non-verbal signals in an awkward or poorly timed way and may speak in a rather monotonous tone of voice. Some may have difficulty in getting the level of familiarity right. They may be excessively formal or, conversely, treat a virtual stranger as an intimate friend.

People at the mild end of the spectrum are often acutely aware of their own difficulties and may be desperate to make friends. They may see others talking but not grasp the informal understandings that underlie such social chat. This can be very frustrating for them. The problem may become more acute in adolescence when friendships are increasingly based on mutual empathy and shared understanding. Frequent, unsuccessful attempts to make friends and continuing demands to deal with people can be very stressful. This may lead to aggressive behaviour and to depression. Such individuals often demonstrate or verbalize little awareness of their own feelings (just as they may be unaware of the feelings of others). Even if they do recognize their own feelings they may not realize that others might be interested, sympathetic and able to help.

How to help

(i) The person with mild ASD may need to be taught explicitly rules and conventions which most people pick up intuitively. Examples might include how to greet people, ways of turn-taking or ending a conversation and how to tell if the other person is interested in the topic.

(ii) It may be necessary to model normal conversational styles for the child with mild ASD with feedback which helps raise awareness of particular strategies and conventions. A framework, such as that provided by Wendy Rinaldi in 'The Social Use of Language Programme', may be helpful in breaking down the skills of conversation into manageable targets. It is worth remembering that the didactic style often used by teachers when talking to a whole class is not actually a very good model for conversation.

(iii) If the child talks endlessly about a specific topic, definite limits should be set on when the topic can and cannot be introduced into conversation. A clear signal may be used to remind the child. It is important to promote the tolerance and understanding of others towards the child with ASD by encouraging other children to engage with them.

(iv) The child may function better in formal activities with some degree of structure, such as clubs involving organized recreational or educational activities. Exposure to less structured contact with other children may need to be supervised. The involvement of younger children in organized playground games is a way of increasing levels of social contact while providing a degree of structure.

(v) The person with ASD needs to be helped to sense warning signs and to anticipate problem situations. In school it is vital to work with the pupil's classmates to help the person with ASD make sense of difficulties which arise. Classmates can also be involved in informal 'Buddy systems' or more formal approaches such as Circle Time.

2 Residual language difficulties

People with mild ASD often have good memories (particularly for facts) and occasionally have special talents with music, maths and drawing. They can also acquire extensive vocabularies. This may lead people to over-estimate their understanding of language and particularly their ability to cope with abstract concepts. In fact, people with ASD are often concrete in their thinking and understanding of language. Attending to instructions or explanations in group settings seems particularly difficult. They may not be 'tuning into' the relevant aspects of what's going on or may be distracted by inessential details. The longer the explanation or instruction and the more abstract the underlying ideas, the more difficult it is for children with mild ASD to comprehend. They often have a literal understanding of language. Metaphor and innuendo may be interpreted literally. The social difficulties experienced by children with mild ASD may also affect comprehension. Even if they understand the actual words they may not be able to grasp the speaker's underlying meaning or intentions. There is a particular problem with sarcasm where people may say one thing with their speech and another with their intonation. This makes people with ASD very vulnerable to teasing, even those at the mild end of the spectrum.

People with mild ASD may have little understanding of what other people are thinking or feeling and so do not comprehend that their behaviour may embarrass someone they are with. They are likely to have difficulty recognizing subtle emotions. They may not have learned the social norms of communication implicitly, as most people do. They are unlikely to appreciate that their social behaviour is out of place and inappropriate. Excessive volume may be an indicator that the person with ASD is anxious in that situation.

How to help

(i) Make sure the person is attending before starting an interaction using their name regularly to reinforce continued attention.

(ii) Think about explanations and instructions; it is helpful to summarize the main points in advance and provide lists. Aide memoires are particularly important for people with subtle language difficulties.

(iii) Monitor your pace of speaking and build in pauses to allow 'processing time' for the child to absorb the information.

(iv) Young people with ASD may be helped by visual cues. Some information and concepts can be represented in pictorial form, diagrams and mind maps.

(v) Though it is a difficult challenge, it is best to keep language as simple as possible. Use short, direct sentences with explicit links between ideas. Be prepared to rephrase if necessary. If specialist or abstract/non-literal language is going to be used, explain it separately, before the person meets it in a work situation.

(vi) When dealing with any misbehaviour it is best to keep a neutral tone and use simple language. It is important to say clearly what has been done wrong, explaining the preferred behaviour with consequences made clear. Long explanations about why a particular behaviour was wrong and attempts to reason with the child may be counterproductive.

(vii) Is the child's hearing normal? This may need to be checked. Model the 'normal' volume that you would like the person to use and provide opportunities for practise.

3 Coping with the unexpected

Many children with mild ASD still need routines. They may organize their lives around structure and routine for themselves. Changes to routines can cause anxiety.

The person may be frightened by the uncertainty of not being able to predict what comes next. Unexpected events can still cause panic. However, some people with ASD at the less severe end of the spectrum appear to accept really major changes, such as a move to a new house or a foreign holiday, while not being able to cope with smaller scale changes so easily.

How to help

(i) Go along with the person's need for routines. Use a timetable to help structure activities. At the same time promote flexibility, such as time for choices and leisure.

(ii) Give advanced warning of changes in routine which are likely to cause frustration. Prepare the child for times when there will be an inevitable wait for a bus or a train.

4 Emotional difficulties: developing self-control

The emotional development of children with ASD tends to proceed at a slower pace. They will often react in a way which is typical of much younger children. Some children with mild ASD show greater than average levels of frustration because of their inability to express adequately their feelings or make sense of everyday social situations. Most people with ASD have problems in understanding the motives and intentions of others. They find coping with other people, particularly in less structured situations, stressful. Sometimes, this tension can boil over in the form of frustrated outbursts. They are less motivated by what other people think of them and may not understand how their behaviour looks (or feels) from someone else's perspective. This may make them less likely to inhibit their own behaviour. Angry outbursts are sometimes a reaction to the frustrations and disappointments they experience in this area.

Some children with ASD will dwell on things that have happened, or relive incidents that may have taken place some time ago. They may become fixated on real or imagined wrongs; this may then spill out as quite an intense delayed reaction. Some are susceptible to fluctuating mood swings, which could be connected to obsessional thoughts or behaviours or may be due to external sensory experiences, such as noise or light. Some children seem to follow a cyclical pattern which determines their moods. Many, even with mild ASD, will not easily develop the social awareness which inhibits most people's behaviour and may show their frustration if made to wait or defer their wishes.

People with mild ASD seem to reach a point of development where they are aware that they are different from others. This often follows a period of time where they have seen differences between themselves and others, but played down or blamed others for these. This realization of 'difference' sometimes occurs while they are still at primary school. However, for the majority it occurs during adolescence and while they are attending secondary school. The decision about whether or not the child should be told of their condition must be left to the child's parents. However, this is something which may need to be raised with the parents if there is reason to believe that it is becoming an issue. If a child is to be told, then further advice can be gained from other professionals about the best way of preparing and supporting the child or adolescent.

How to help

(i) It may be useful to look for triggers to see if any of these can be avoided or modified, for example, noisy places and echoing buildings such as swimming pools. It may be easier to avoid such problems than to change the person's basic style of thinking and feeling.

(ii) The person with ASD will need help to recognize when beginning to feel upset. There may be a need for effective self-calming strategies or the person may simply require a routine for getting away from situations where a loss of self-control seems likely. This will need to be rehearsed and when introduced into 'real-life' situations the person will need to be given cues.

(iii) It is important to de-brief the person after incidents. This should be separated from any sanction that is imposed so that the discussion can be kept calm, simple and factual. Focus should be on identifying the early stages of the incident and looking at ways in which the difficulty might have been resolved or avoided.

(iv) Offer incentives and rewards for self-control.

(v) Develop the child's emotional vocabulary. Interpret how you think the child is feeling and give the feeling a name. The child will gradually build a memory store of emotional experiences and will develop a more general concept of what leads to each emotion and what it feels like.

(vi) If the child is highly obsessional set aside times during the day when this can be accommodated. Obsessions and routines are often driven by anxiety. Attempts to eradicate them will inevitably lead to greater frustration.

(vii) If the mood swings seem to be cyclical and have no apparent external cause the person may need medical help. The child could be suffering from clinical depression, which is not uncommon in children with ASD who have a degree of self-awareness.

(viii) Don't expect the child with ASD spontaneously to discuss emotions and feelings. Even with a high level of self-awareness it may be that there is no appreciation that others can be interested in their welfare.

5 Anxiety and depression

People with mild ASD frequently feel very anxious. Many aspects of life, taken for granted by those without the condition, are frightening and bewildering for them. Many of the reactions typical of a child with mild ASD can be seen as reactions connected with high anxiety. Inappropriate behaviour, over the top reactions, excessive fear, aggression and panic are all familiar reactions. It is important to consider many of the bizarre reactions of the child in the light of the anxiety and stress they encounter; the responses of others need to be shaped accordingly.

Many children with mild ASD repeatedly experience failure or rejection in social situations. What others seem to do naturally requires great effort on their part and even then, their attempts to 'read' others may not be successful. The management of some children with ASD in a school can be very time consuming and demanding. Such children have difficulty understanding how others think and feel. They often put a great deal of effort into this and become upset when they fail. Some people with ASD become aware that they are different. They often become depressed about this since they would prefer to be like others.

How to help

(i) In order to reduce anxieties provide predictability, stability and a consistent daily routine. The person should be forewarned of any changes in expected routine so there is good preparation.

(ii) Irrational fears usually respond to gradual de-sensitization. This involves giving the child the chance to encounter and deal with their fears in a controlled setting where the child is in control.

(iii) Novel activities, such as swimming, horse riding or visits to new places, may need very careful introduction. It is necessary to be as concrete as possible in describing them and to check the child's understanding.

(iv) Teach strategies for relieving or controlling anxiety. Some commercially available stress-reducing toys can be helpful, as can various relaxation techniques.

(v) In school, ensure that someone has responsibility for actively monitoring the person's well-being and for providing opportunities to discuss concerns and feelings. The person with mild ASD may not be aware of the significance of the diagnosis or realize that it could be helpful to talk to someone.

(vi) Involve the person in monitoring self-behaviour, in which good and unhappy days are identified and seeing what has contributed to any pattern that emerges. Try to develop a set of positive rewards which can be used when the person is feeling low.

(vii) Be alert to evidence of more serious difficulty. Watch out for signs of deterioration in attentiveness, self-organization, and increased stress and isolation. If need be, take steps to involve outside help. Parents will need to discuss the situation with their GP. Teachers may wish to discuss this further with an educational psychologist.

6 Personal organization

Children with ASD often seem to have great difficulty with personal organization. They can appear to be overloaded and confused by having to cope simultaneously with language, perceptual stimulation and social demands. This can happen to all of us in certain circumstances, but people with ASD seem to have a much lower threshold. The young person with mild ASD may fail to see the point of making the extra effort needed for personal organization, the motive to please people or get work finished, or to master particular skills may be poorly developed. These organizational problems show themselves at a number of different levels, for example, in knowing where to stand in open spaces and how to get from A to B; knowing where to put answers on worksheets or how to organize drawings and text on a blank page; having the right materials for the right lessons or task; and knowing what to bring from home and take home on a given day.

How to help

(i) Make a list, which is readily accessible, of what the child needs each day. Prompt its use if necessary.

(ii) Ensure any assignment is clearly understood. Provide all the necessary equipment and ensure the child knows where it should be kept. Coloured boxes are helpful. If the child has a written assignment make it apparent where the answers should go by marking this area with boundaries or colours.

(iii) The child could be given a map for getting around the environment, neighbourhood and school.

7 **Classroom skills**

Many people with mild ASD also have fine motor problems which makes writing challenging for them. Some may be able to write well at the beginning of an activity but quickly become tired. Others demonstrate greater difficulties with handwriting. There may also be difficulty in working to a specified time limit so that a task may not always be completed in the time required.

Some children with mild ASD cannot cope with homework because it muddles the boundary between home and school which confuses them. Many cannot see the point in homework even though they can verbalize why it should be completed, (for example, to gain better coursework marks, to show effort and hard work, because it is a school rule). Some children with ASD will try to give a reason for not producing homework. This may have been valid on one occasion but they may continue to offer it each time, whether appropriate or not. Most will produce some homework, often on topics they find interesting, but may have difficulties meeting time limits due to poor personal organization skills.

How to help

(i) While it is important for the young person to develop handwriting skills this is not the only method of recording. Alternatives which can be explored include the use of computer; iPad; dictating responses to another person; cutting and sticking material by way of illustration.

(ii) The person with ASD needs to know how much is expected in the working environment. They may have difficulties in predicting what output is usual or acceptable. In some cases it may be helpful to use markers of time passing, such as sand timers or a large clock face. These will give the pupil a visual prompt.

(iii) Parents and teachers should collaborate over ways to help motivate and organize the child. A meeting to set up a homework policy may be helpful, which should include parents.

The causes of ASD

Despite the powerful modern genetic techniques available to researchers there are a number of obstacles to gaining a full understanding of the genetic basis of autism. It is possible that what is classed under the umbrella of autism may in fact be a number of distinct conditions, each with a different underlying genetic cause. If this is the case then by grouping the distinct conditions together it will be difficult to find strong genetic determinants that underlie each of them separately. With the development of more sophisticated tools it may become possible to separate patients into distinct sub-categories of autism that could then be considered separately in different genetic studies.

Neil Walsh and Elisabeth Hurley

ALL THAT MATTERS

▶ Introduction

Since its identification, research into ASD has accelerated. Many journals (see 100 Ideas) have emerged dedicated solely to the welter of research. Identifying the causes of ASD has been a major preoccupation since informing treatment and possible prevention are the major aims of any research programme. One of the original, most distressing and misguided notions about ASD was that the cause was a mother being particularly cold and unresponsive to her baby. This was termed the 'refrigerator mother' theory; the refrigerator father escaped investigation. This theory largely arose from the work of Bruno Bettelheim who had a psychoanalytical training, which emphasized the importance of attachment in psychological development. Theories about the causes of ASD have been numerous; some have been promising and some frankly implausible. Examples of the more contentious explanations proposed (and in one case, its refutation) can be seen in newspaper reports.

Doctors link autism to MMR vaccination

Independent 27.02.98

MMR scare research withdrawn by *Lancet* Medical Journal

Independent 03.02.10

The decline in MMR vaccinations had disastrous consequences. In 2013 the press reported the death of a man following a measles epidemic. The headline stated:

Measles outbreak: number of cases passes 1,000 in Swansea area. Man dies.

Guardian 30.04.13

Other examples of possible causes of ASD have also been reported:

Vinyl flooring doubles the chances of children being autistic
Indepenent 05.04.09

Rise of autism may be linked to Western diet
Independent 04.07.13

Low IQ and autism risk from fertility treatment for men with poor sperm
Daily Mail 03.07.13

There is general agreement among experts in the field that ASD results from atypical brain or neurological functioning present from birth. Although the causes of the dysfunction may be various, the result is the abnormal development and behavioural responses characteristic of autism. Exact mechanisms and supposed differences in brain function and structure remain elusive; it was originally assumed that there was one common site of dysfunction in the brain but as research has progressed it has become evident that there are many different sites implicated in various different forms of the disorder. Genetic factors, maternal disease and toxic environmental factors and interactions between these have all been implicated as causes.

Research has shown that there is no one common site of dysfunction but there are similar observable consequences resulting from dysfunction occurring in various areas of the brain. Accordingly, there may be many distinct neurological pathways leading to the same behavioural consequences. A range of different underlying neurological deficits give rise to typical ASD behaviours. These deficits result in problems with language, socialization, and restricted and repetitive behaviours thus meeting all the criteria for a diagnosis of ASD. In this regard a parallel is drawn between the concept of ASD and severe ID. Children with severe ID often have well-defined rare syndromes involving different types of brain dysfunction but resulting in similar behaviours and cognitive deficits.

Given that the behavioural symptoms commonly associated with autism may result from a variety of different causes, it is unsurprising that in all the psychological and neurological studies only a proportion of subjects with ASD show the particular features under investigation. That is, not all ASD children fail the Sally–Anne test for a Theory of Mind (see Chapter 10) and not all children with ASD have observable brain function differences.

The search for one cause for ASD has been abandoned and many commentators are now using 'Autism Spectrum Disorders' or 'The Autisms' (Coleman and Gillberg), in the plural, reflecting a multiplicity of disorders but having common behavioural features. DSM-4 used the singular for both Asperger's Disorder and Autistic Disorder suggesting one discernible and discrete disorder. However, over the last 15 years what has emerged is a multiplicity of candidate mutated genes, chromosome defects and interacting environmental triggers. Researchers are also beginning to report on clusters of behavioural features occurring in ASD children such as severely autistic children with echolalia and mildly autistic children with hand flapping, suggesting that there are discernible distinct subgroups under the ASD umbrella.

ASD is regularly reported to co-exist with a large number of other conditions. Co-morbid conditions include children with a wide range of chromosome and genetic defects, especially tuberous sclerosis, homocystinuria, Prader-Willi syndrome, Fragile X syndrome, Angelman syndrome and Timothy syndrome, as well as children with non-verbal syndrome and children with epilepsy. In addition, children who have suffered very severe neglect have also been found to present with autistic-like traits. Romanian orphans, who were the victims of severe emotional and physical neglect, were studied by the eminent psychiatrist Michael Rutter in 1999 who described them as having 'quasi-autism'.

▶ Environmental and maternal disease factors in ASD

There is some evidence that ASD may also result from the various environmental conditions that can affect development in utero. It has long been known that maternal viral infections such as rubella can have a devastating effect on the developing embryo early in pregnancy. Equally, certain drugs and, notoriously, thalidomide, can interfere with the development of the foetus. ID has been shown to have positive correlations with a range of perinatal factors including hypertension in pregnancy, maternal asthma, maternal urinary tract infection, ante-partum haemorrhage, poor foetal growth and maternal infections. However, the picture is not so clear for ASD. Some studies have reported that threatened abortion before 20 weeks, gestation and poor foetal growth were associated with an increased risk of children with intellectual disabilities also having a diagnosis of ASD. However, other retrospective studies have not found any significant prenatal factors associated with children who were tested as having average range intelligence and diagnosed with ASD. Baron-Cohen reports on another possible environmental factor and ASD. It has been found that the extent of exposure to testosterone in the womb ('prenatal testosterone') is related to the development of autistic-like traits in the general population.

Exposure to prenatal infection has been suggested to cause deficiencies in foetal neurodevelopment especially in the early months. In one study, all children born in Denmark between 1980 and 2005 were screened. Diagnoses of ASD and maternal infection were obtained through nationwide registers and the data was analysed. Admission to hospital due to maternal viral infection in the first trimester and maternal bacterial infection in the second trimester were found to be associated with an increased risk of a diagnosis of ASD in the child. These results supported the hypotheses that early prenatal infection in the mother increased the risk of ASD in her child. It seems likely that exposure to certain toxic factors in the early months of pregnancy, including certain viruses, can affect the developing foetus and lead to ASD.

A contentious theory has also been developed by Michael Goldberg in the USA into the relationship between the high proportion of children reported to have allergies and immune deficiency diseases and ASD. He believes that autism is a symptom of a treatable viral disease that attacks the brain's immune system in infancy.[52] While there is evidence for the effects of prenatal, genetic factors, there is minimal evidence that children could be susceptible to developing ASD from a disease acquired after birth. Moreover, allergies and immune deficiency diseases are more common in children with known genetic diseases.

▶ Genetic research and ASD

Genes act like a recipe or blueprint that control growth, development and how our bodies work. Genes are made up of long strings of DNA, groups of which are packaged tightly into chromosomes. Humans are made up of billions of cells, almost all of which contain a complete set of about 30,000 genes and a full set of 46 chromosomes in the nucleus of every cell.

Genes contain information for producing proteins that build all the cells in our bodies. However, the gene can be faulty either through inheritance or by a chance change (*de novo*). Faulty genes are called mutations. The information contained in the faulty gene leads to changes in the structure of a protein which can affect the function of particular cells. It was hypothesized that changes of this nature result in changes to the biochemistry and structure of the brain and a simple genetic mutation could result in ASD. For example, the fact that autism affects males four times more often than females suggests that there may be genes on the sex-determining chromosome (X) that can predispose someone to autism. The search began for atypical genes that might be implicated.

Family history studies show that some of the autism-like symptoms, such as delays in language development, occur more often in parents, brothers and sisters of people with autism than in families who have no autistic relatives. These studies confirmed that autism is linked to genetic inheritance because members of the same family have similar genes.

Studies of twins have established that monozygotic or identical twins show a higher incidence of autism than dizygotic twins but reports of concordance rates vary. When one twin of an identical twin pair has autism, the other twin does not always develop the condition, which suggests that there are likely to be 'environmental factors' that are also necessary to trigger ASD. Without these triggers, the condition may not develop. It may be that there is a genetic (inherited) predisposition to developing autism triggered by other unknown factors.

It was soon evident, therefore, that the picture was far more complex than the occurrence of one or two mutated genes being responsible for ASD. In his book *Zero Degrees of Empathy* (2011), Simon Baron-Cohen describes the existence of what he calls 'a genetic signature' in some families where one member has ASD. He states that such families frequently show more than average autistic traits in other family members. His research team has looked at candidate genes associated with ASD. He concludes that there are many genes now identified, which appear to have a role in autism. At least three genes have been identified affecting how the brain responds to emotional recognition and emotional expression, for example.

Based on all these findings, there is growing evidence of a link between atypical genes and autism. However, as Baron-Cohen acknowledges, it is a big jump from identifying candidate genes to understanding how their functions have an impact on development and behaviour. Because of the wide variability of intellectual and behavioural patterns of people with ASD, researchers believe that 'autisms' can result from many different gene mutations. Moreover, these interact with each other and with environmental triggers. To complicate the picture further, emerging information about epigenetics may lead us to a new understanding of inheritance. It has long been held that our traits are hardwired in the DNA that passes from parent to offspring but it would appear that some new traits resulting from interactions with the environment can also be inherited. The picture is highly complex but all the evidence shows that some children have a genetic susceptibility to autism. What makes some susceptible and others not is an important research question.

While investigations are still at an early stage, certain genes have now been identified which appear to be involved in particular functions in the body. These include genes involved in neural development and neural transmission. Neuroimaging studies of adults with ASD have shown some evidence of altered connectivity, suggesting a degree of atypical 'wiring' in the brain. There is evidence suggesting a role for certain genes in neural growth, neural patterning and the action of synapses (the connection between neurons) within the brain. It is argued that mutated genes might play a defining role in producing atypical patterns of neural connectivity. This may result in symptoms evident in ASD.

In view of the abnormalities in social behaviour seen in ASD, an increasing number of studies have focused on genes known to be involved in social behaviour and emotions. The hormone oxytocin is known to be involved in neural transmission and the regulation of emotion. The oxytocin receptor gene, OXTR, is one of the candidate genes that has been shown to be associated with ASD in multiple studies.

A study reported by Abrahams and Geschwind in 2008 compared genes linked with autism to those of other neurological diseases and found that more than half of known autism genes are implicated in other disorders. This suggests that the other disorders such as Fragile X syndrome and 15q duplication may share mechanisms with autism. The Simons Foundation (Sfari) has an interesting website that seeks to keep people abreast of developments in genetic research.

Hundreds of genes have now been the subject of research into ASD and a number of 'bona fide risk genes' identified (see 100 Ideas section for a list of some candidates). The task is enormous. Once a link is identified replication studies are necessary but sometimes promising findings are not replicated. Findings from research support an emerging consensus within the scientific community that autism is caused in part by many 'rare variants' or genetic changes found in less than one per cent of the population. While each of these mutations may only account for a small fraction of the cases, collectively they are starting to amount to a greater percentage of individuals with ASD, as well as providing insights into possible common dysfunctional mechanisms. The overlap between autism susceptibility genes and those previously implicated in intellectual disabilities further supports the hypothesis that at least some genetic risk factors are shared by different developmental disabilities. Finally, identification of biological pathways points to new avenues of scientific investigation, as well as potential targets for the development of new interventions.

Chromosome abnormalities

There are then faulty genes which have been identified and implicated in ASD. In addition, problems with the structure of chromosomes are also being identified. Genes are carried on microscopically small, thread-like structures called chromosomes. There are 46 chromosomes in the human genome, 23 inherited from our mother and 23 from our father, so we have sets of chromosomes in pairs. Apart from two sex chromosomes (two Xs for a girl and XY for a boy on the 23rd chromosome) the chromosomes are numbered from 1 to 22 from the largest to smallest. Each chromosome has a short arm (p) and a long arm (q) (for example, in the diagram below in image 7 p is the top part and q is the bottom part).

Normal Human Karyotype

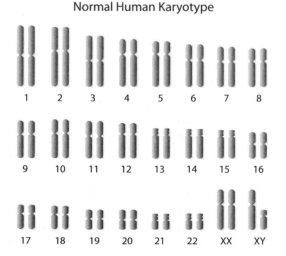

Aberrations in chromosomes can occur when the structure is disrupted. For example, one of the arms can be deleted, the arms can be translocated or there can be duplications of whole or part of a chromosome arm.

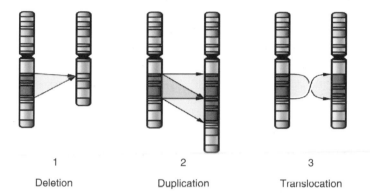

1	2	3
Deletion	Duplication	Translocation

These aberrations can either be inherited or can occur by chance (*de novo*) without a family history. People with changes in the number or structure of their chromosomes may have an increased risk of a range of birth defects, developmental delay, behavioural problems, ID and/or ASD.

At the turn of the millennium, up to 2,000 chromosome abnormalities had been detected by cytogenetic analysis using a technique called the FISH test (Fluorescence In Situ Hybridization). Using a fluorescence microscope and computer software a comparison can be made between normal healthy chromosomes and aberrant ones. Since 2000, and partly as a result of The Human Genome Project, a technique called Array Comparative Genomic Hybridization (CGH) has been increasingly available. Array CGH is mainly used to detect genetic abnormalities in cancer. However, it is also suitable for the analysis of chromosome abnormalities that cause disorders. Array CGH is employed to uncover deletions, duplications, translocations, breakpoints and other abnormalities in chromosomes. Array CGH is much more sensitive than the earlier tests in detecting submicroscopic aberrations. It is now possible to detect tiny micro deletions or duplications and offer genetic counselling. Array CGH will not detect all abnormalities but it is a huge step forward and one that has major implications for medical ethics. This means that many more children will get an accurate diagnosis from Array CGH analysis than from the older FISH test.

At present we do not know the function and impact of many of our genes and chromosomes or the role that epigenetics might play so it is not possible to predict what the consequence is of having a particular gene or chromosome abnormality. Additionally:

▶ Even if a candidate gene is thought to be responsible for a particular feature it does not always mean that the associated feature will be present

▶ Other genetic and environmental factors often have a role in determining the presence or absence of a particular feature

▶ The amount of genetic material that is duplicated or deleted varies and the impact of the aberration seems to be proportional to the disruption

It should be remembered that the majority of cases of ASD are likely to be due to multiple factors and there are individuals with genetic abnormalities who do not have an ASD diagnosis. A diagnosis of an aberrant mutation is not equivalent to a diagnosis of ASD even when there is a strong association; knowing the genetic defect does not provide a predictive description of the child's behaviours.

▶ Abnormalities in brain structure and ASD

Over the last few decades great advances have been made in our understanding of the way brains work and the areas of the brain involved in normal functioning. The original work on how the brain and its components function was often conducted as the result of brain injury. For example, it had previously been established that injury to the prefrontal cortex could disrupt the personality and higher-level functioning. Technological advances in scanning have enabled researchers to look into the intact working brain and to map functions.

ASD results from brain dysfunction but not all people with ASD manifest the same symptoms and not all show the same abnormalities of brain structure. However, recent promising research has identified that a significant proportion of children with ASD have larger brains with thicker cortices. This finding has led to hypotheses about connectivity differences in neural processing. Post-mortem studies, for example, have shown characteristic differences in minicolumns in autistic subjects. Minicolumns are multiples of neurons working together in a concerted fashion.

An alternative line of enquiry, discussed by the psychiatrist Digby Tantam in 2009, suggests that autistic individuals may possess a defect in mirroring or copying actions performed by others. Cells in the brain which appear to specialize in these functions have been identified and differences between subjects with ASD and controls discovered. In the 1990s, Rizzolatti and his colleagues examined the response of single cells in the prefrontal cortex when a monkey moved its hand to grasp a grape. They discovered that when the monkey observed a human experimenter reaching out to grasp the grape, the monkey's neurons also fired. These mirror neurons respond to the monkey's own actions *and* similar actions of others. The neurons of the monkey function in a system lacking language. The mirror neurons are located in an area in the monkey's brain similar to that in the human brain known to be involved in speech. This might indicate that these neurons have evolved in humans to allow us to make a prediction about another's intentions. Subsequent studies have found areas in the human brain which are similarly activated when observing and implementing movements. This system may be disrupted or damaged in the autistic individual.

Baron-Cohen and colleagues have established a great deal of evidence to show that areas of the brain known to be involved with empathic responding are underactive in a proportion of children and adults with ASD. They have proposed that there is an 'empathy circuit' within the brain which is normally involved in being able to view the world from someone else's perspective, co-operative social interaction and even self-reflection all of which are impaired in autism.

In 2010, researchers from the Institute of Psychiatry at King's College London aimed to test the theory that individuals with autism have multidimensional differences in brain shape, structure and volume. They devised a computer program to measure these differences. The researchers recruited participants including 20 adults who had been diagnosed with ASD and a further 20 adults without the condition as a control group. The diagnosis of ASD was confirmed using accepted behavioural criteria. In addition, 19 adults diagnosed with ADHD were also recruited to act as a neurodevelopmental control group to see whether the method could differentiate between ASD and other neurodevelopmental disorders. The researchers used MRI to take scans of the participants' brains in all three groups.

The study was able to identify individuals with ASD with an accuracy of up to 90 per cent (i.e. if the subject had a clinical diagnosis of ASD, there was a 90 per cent probability that he or she was correctly assigned to the ASD category by the computer program). However, the accuracy of the results varied according to the measurements used. For example, the highest accuracy of 90 per cent was obtained using a measurement of cortical thickness in the left hemisphere. On the right hemisphere, the assessments were not as accurate. Of the control group, 80 per cent were correctly classified as not having a clinical diagnosis of ASD. In the ADHD group, information from the left hemisphere was more accurate in predicting the condition and in differentiating between ADHD and ASD.

Arguably, this approach could diminish the need for the time-consuming process of interviewing parents and family members and eliminate the subjectivity of their responses. Along with genetic analysis, this technique offers the prospect of an altogether objective and incontrovertible test for ASD. However, there are many obstacles to be overcome before this technique is readily available and of proven reliability, not least being able to get young children to co-operate with having a brain scan. The claim for a swift method of diagnosis, therefore, may be somewhat exaggerated and premature. Importantly, ASD is not a single entity with one structural presentation.

At the same time new drugs are being developed which may alter brain chemistry and ameliorate some of the difficulties related to the difficult aspects of ASD behaviour such as anxiety and hyperactivity. Trials of oxytocin on a small sample of high-functioning autistic people had a positive effect with regard to patterns of social interaction. However, there is no miracle pill for ASD. There are no specific drugs for the disorder and the NAS has warned that since there are many causes of autism, drugs may have only limited effect on particular people.

10

Theories about the effects of autism on thinking

'We don't know why Sam (now aged 11) can remember things so vividly. Nor why he can hear sounds that are beyond most people's range; why he can read with phenomenal concentration yet cannot write his own name. We don't understand why he finds some things so frightening; why he becomes anxious when routines change; why he has such intense and focused interests; why he struggles to recognise members of his family, most importantly neither does he. No one can tell us what it all means.'

Clare Lawrence

ALL THAT
MATTERS

Although geneticists and neurobiologists have now taken the lead in research in a field once dominated by psychiatrists and psychologists, there are different but complementary levels of explanation. Psychologists are interested in behaviour, cognition and development and have approached ASD from this perspective. They have tried to understand the thinking processes of people with ASD and how these differ from non-autistic people. This has been vital in developing ways of teaching and intervening. Some psychological theories have been seen to have real explanatory power and some of these are now reviewed.

▶ Theory of Mind or 'mind blindness'

Theory of Mind describes the ability of someone to see the world through the eyes of another and understand how they may be feeling or why they are acting in a particular way. Children as young as four can tell white lies, use double bluff, act deceptively and maintain false beliefs. They understand that the person receiving the lie is fooled because they can take the imaginative leap of standing in that individual's shoes. It is something that delights children of this age. The ability to engage in these activities is referred to as 'mentalizing'. Infants with autism show delayed or absent development of mentalizing. They are often unable to take the perspective of another person and to understand that others have their own minds. This is also referred to as mind blindness.

In 1983, two psychologists, Heinz Wimmer and Joseph Perner, created a false belief task in order to test a child's Theory of Mind, now termed the 'Sally–Anne Task'. A scene is set up which the child views involving two small dolls or puppets (Sally and Anne). Sally puts a marble into her basket and leaves the room. Anne moves the marble from the basket to her box. Sally comes back into the room. The child watching this scene is then asked, 'Where will Sally look for her marble?' This task requires the child to recognize that a deception has occurred and that Sally will not know that the marble has been moved. Most young children predict that Sally will believe that the marble is in her basket where she left it. Most young children with ASD state that the marble is in Anne's box. Essentially, in order to succeed at the task, the child has to be aware that different people can hold different beliefs about a situation even when they may actually be mistaken.

In subsequent studies conducted by Simon Baron-Cohen, it was found that 80 per cent of children with autism failed the test, as compared with non-autistic children and children with Down's syndrome where over 80 per cent passed. The results were suggestive that children with ASD as a group fail to employ a Theory of Mind. There appears to be an inability to understand the mental states of others. This puts people with ASD at a grave disadvantage when having to predict the behaviour of other people. Without doubt, since this original work, difficulties with mentalizing and Theory of Mind have become a cornerstone of research into autism and cognitive processes.

The neurological basis for Theory of Mind has been investigated and discussed by the psychologist Uta Frith.

She reported on studies of adults with ASD, compared with control groups, doing various mentalizing tasks while their brains were scanned using functional MRI (fMRI). She concluded that the connectivity between the visual- and emotion-registering regions in the brain was weaker in the autistic group than in the controls. The apparent mind blindness in autism could be due to restricted information flow between areas of the brain.

There is distinctive heterogeneity of ASD individuals; not all autistic children and adults have mind blindness. For example, high-functioning autistic children and adults often pass tests of mentalizing. Individuals with autism can come to understand mental states. However, their mentalizing ability is not intuitive, and they must actively work out another's perspective. Similarly, mentalizing problems are not entirely specific to autism. Deaf and blind individuals have also been found to perform poorly on Theory of Mind tasks. It has also been pointed out that there are other impairments in autism, such as restricted and repetitive behaviours, fear of change and motor mannerisms which are not explained by a problem of mind blindness.

▶ Baron-Cohen's Empathizing/Systemizing (E/S) Theory and ASD

In more recent research Baron-Cohen and his colleagues have developed another theory of autism based on earlier work on gender differences. This research has shown that there are gender-related differences to the way that males and females respond to emotions in others. Baron-Cohen states that:

Empathising is the drive to identify another person's emotions and thoughts and to respond to these with an appropriate emotion.... Systemising is the drive to analyse and explore a system and to extract underlying rules.

Females have been found to be more sensitive to facial expression, while males are more interested in subjects such as engineering involving underlying structures.

Using research findings, Baron-Cohen suggests that females are generally more empathetic and men are more typically systemizers. According to his theory, females are often person-centred and intuitively aware of how someone else is feeling while men are better at investigating how underlying rules and structures operate such as categorizing and ordering data. He continues by claiming that the female brain is 'predominantly hardwired for empathy' and the male brain is 'predominantly hardwired for understanding and building systems'. This is termed the empathizing/ systemizing theory (E/S theory). Baron-Cohen argues that these differences were related to production of the male sex hormone testosterone.

Exposure to abnormally high levels of testosterone in utero has been linked to autism. Children with autism demonstrate many of the male characteristics identified by Baron-Cohen. They often show the same sort of preoccupation with understanding how systems work. They frequently enjoy ordering collections of objects or data; show interest in encyclopaedias; and have preoccupations with such things as washing machines, catalogues, timetables, technical manuals, and schedules. These differences were found to exist across cultures. The obsessional interests that people with ASD often show focus on a system with an underlying structured pattern. The child may be focusing on the details of a system in order to work out the underlying rules that govern it.

The characteristic approach of the person with ASD is to become obsessed with the minutiae of a subject. Their learning style is to prefer a narrow, obsessional interest explored in depth. The child with ASD may have strengths with systemizing but they usually have impaired empathizing. Baron-Cohen has also turned his attention to savant syndrome and suggests that the special skills, such as calendar calculation, musical ability, drawing in linear perspective, are all particular examples of systemizing in action. These special skills require the application of complex rules and predictable structures. An 'extreme male brain' may account for some of the classic diagnostic features of ASD.

Further research using brain imaging shows that people with ASD frequently show under-activity in areas of the brain believed to be involved in sympathetic attitudes and responses to others. When asked to make judgements about intentions, motives or the state of mind of others, they show reduced activity in areas of the brain known to be involved in emotional responses.

▶ Weak central coherence theory

Following on from the development of Theory of Mind as being one of the central deficits in ASD, Uta Frith and her colleagues have suggested that individuals with ASD have weak central coherence. This is a term which describes the tendency for non-autistic individuals to process information using its context to access meaning. In contrast people with ASD demonstrate 'local processing', whereby details and parts of information are the focus. For example, children with ASD approach a block design task (see below) with their focus of interest on the individual pieces and sections of the puzzle. This appears to give them a particular facility in completing the whole. Average children tend to focus on the whole rather than the parts.

Original pattern

Segmented pattern

Type of blocks available for making the pattern

▲ The child is given three-dimensional blocks as illustrated and asked to complete the image using four of the blocks

Non-autistic children proceed in exactly the opposite manner, moving from a global outline to incidental detail. In terms of linguistic skills, it has been noted that autistic children could recite fragments of a story or narrative with precision but were unable to explain the gist of the story. They often cannot integrate the fragments easily into a coherent narrative, which is a relatively easy task for normally developing children.

Earlier theorists had tended to focus on deficits in ASD, such as poor social interaction and problems with a Theory of Mind. But weak central coherence theory can also account for some strengths. Uta Frith and her colleagues found that children with ASD were faster than matched controls in identifying a hidden figure in a picture because they attended to detail.

Weak central coherence: deficit or strength?

Autistic individuals are less likely to succumb to standard visual illusions, conjuring tricks and other events that might bemuse a non-autistic child. Francesca Happé presented autistic children with a series of visual illusions, such as the Titchener circles.

In non-autistic individuals the presence of the surrounding circles affects the ability to judge whether the two inner circles are really the same size. Autistic subjects appear to perceive such figures in a less unified, more piecemeal way and are, therefore, less likely to succumb to the illusion. This theory may also help to explain the remarkable ability of some autistic subjects in computation, music and perspective drawing who otherwise show severe impairments in global processing skills particularly with language, communication and social understanding. There are examples of autistic savants such as Nadia, who drew separate details building up a drawing of an object rather than the usual approach of sketching an outline first. Her drawing of a horse illustrates how this was undertaken.

Central coherence theory offers a great deal of evidence for a difference in cognitive style related to ASD. It points to a facility with processing detail, possibly at the expense of context, particularly in visually presented materials but also in processing language. Happé has linked these findings to suggest that the effects may indicate diffuse brain mechanisms and relates this to the finding that some people with ASD appear to have larger brains than normal with increased cell packing in some areas. She speculates that processing with excess neurons may lead to attention to detail rather than a more economical grasp of the gist.

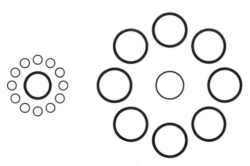

▲ Titchener circles: This is a visual illusion whereby the centre circle on the left appears to be larger than the centre circle on the right. Both centre circles are exactly the same size

▶ Executive dysfunction theory and ASD

Executive functions are the intelligent processes that facilitate new ways of behaving and optimize reactions to unfamiliar circumstances. For example, we engage in such processes when we switch from one activity to another or when we make a plan or change our mind about a situation. Interest in executive functioning and ASD has developed in parallel to weak central coherence theory. It attempts to account for deficits in understanding and to link this closely to underlying neurology. The American psychologist Sally Ozonoff was one of the first to investigate executive functioning in relation to ASD. Insofar as those with ASD show impairments in their ability to plan or to encompass change, especially in unfamiliar surroundings or in new social situations, they could be said to have deficits in executive functioning.

At the heart of most theories about executive functioning is the distinction between what we do automatically, as a well-learned routine, and what we do in a non-routine way when we consciously have to monitor, change and control our behaviour. Routine processing is behaviour that is over-learned and automatic, whereas non-routine behaviour is the processing we have to do when the situation is novel or when our usual responses are not appropriate. Executive functioning allows us to behave appropriately and flexibly.

▲ A line-by-line reconstruction of a horse's head drawn by Nadia, made with the aid of videotaped observation. The order of the drawing reveals her use of segments rather than an overall outline of the head.

Research on executive functioning and the brain

Over the last 30 years great advances have been made in our understanding of neurology and the discrete areas of the brain involved in higher-level executive functioning. Studies using neuroimaging and MRI scanning have been able to map the link between demands made using tasks of executive function and the operation of the prefrontal cortex. Much of our understanding of executive functioning was based on studies of patients with frontal lobe damage. Many of these individuals are found to be impulsive, unable to pursue goals over a long period and defer gratification. In other patients with frontal lobe damage the problem is that they perseverate over simple tasks and appear unable to stop an activity and pursue another. There is, therefore, a fundamental difference between habitual behaviour and intelligent behaviour. Intelligent action is seen as a 'supervisory system' and is the primary function of the frontal lobes. Damage to this system could explain the excessive rigidity, distractibility and impulsivity seen in patients with frontal lobe damage. These behaviours are also observed in people with ASD.

▶ Non-verbal communication and ASD

In his book intriguingly entitled, *Can the World Afford Autistic Spectrum Disorder?* (2009), Tantam has reminded researchers that one of the most devastating and pervasive problems suffered by all children with ASD is their failure to read body language, facial expressions and all the subtle ways we communicate without language via non-verbal communication. He makes the point that social interaction is dependent on two or more people focusing on a task or issue that requires joint attention. Non-verbal communication is essential in social relationships and in comprehending and expressing emotion. Although this deficit is generally recognized as key in ASD, he claims that its significance and importance has been underestimated in recent years.

▶ Conclusions

There are a number of overlapping and interrelated theories about the central cognitive deficits in autism all of which have emerged in the last 30 years and contribute to our understanding of this perplexing and distressing condition. If, as is now proposed, autism is a number of different disorders with a common behavioural presentation then there will be some psychological explanations that do not apply to particular subgroups and individuals and this would account for the fact that only a proportion of children show the particular deficits.

Together with the challenge posed by the lack of homogeneity in ASD, we also have different theories to explain the presenting symptoms. However, all the theories can co-exist, especially since this is a heterogeneous group of people, and some of the theories may be linked by considering them as pertaining to different ages and stages of development. Non-verbal difficulties, such as failing to give eye contact or give joint attention can be demonstrated at a very early stage of development before the infant has any expressive language. A Theory of Mind involves understanding language and instructions and can only be demonstrated after the age of two. Central coherence theory and executive functioning can also be seen as intimately related. Not being able to see the wood for the trees or grasping the general picture must lead to difficulties with decision-making, planning and executive functioning. Very high levels of anxiety are increasingly seen as both a significant problem for people with ASD and as an explanation for some of the classic features of autism such as retreating into obsessional activities and social withdrawal. Most importantly, psychological and genetic research into ASD helps us understand normal cognition. Some theories have emerged that now have a very solid evidence base and move our understanding of ASD and normal development forward.

Conclusions

Some parents and autistic individuals have expressed dissatisfaction with the major investment in basic science research in autism in comparison to interventions. They contend that the emphasis on science research necessarily diverts precious funds and research efforts away from work that they claim is most needed, including research on interventions and services and strategies to help people manage the difficulties they face.

Elizabeth Pellicano and Marc Stears

ALL THAT MATTERS

The overriding concern of all parents is obtaining the best possible future for their children. Parents of a child with ASD have their own unique journey to make and their concern to secure the best education and support is even more acute. Diagnosis is rarely made at birth and the gradual awareness that something is wrong with their child is made over the next two years. Indeed, in some cases the child appears to develop normally during the first two years and may start to develop single words and sentences only to regress. It is as if the language acquired does not lead to meaningful interaction and it can then fade away. There is inevitably an agonizing period when the parents must confront the fact that their beautiful child is not developing normally. A regular feature of ASD is that the child may have flashes of connection. There may be periods of rapid development and long plateaux when no observable progress is made. Parents have often told me that there must be a key that could unlock the door to communication. This is summed up by novelist David Mitchell when he writes about first reading Naoki Higashida, a Japanese boy who can apparently explain what it is like to have severe autism: 'It felt as though for the first time our own son was talking to us about what was happening inside his head, through Naoki's words... it offers up proof that locked inside the helpless-seeming autistic body is a mind as curious, subtle and complex as yours and mine, as anyone's.'

When a child is first diagnosed families often respond with denial and shock and a process of adjustment begins. Families often turn to professionals such as teachers and care workers for advice and support. The

NAS and regional and local associations bring parents into contact with other families as well as providing advice and support. Over the years, parents develop their own network of help including those with similar problems. They are all faced with an obstacle course of decisions, setbacks and triumphs.

Another obstacle faced by parents is obtaining a diagnosis in the first place and then additional provisions such as speech therapy. Resources used to be made available via a Statement of Special Educational Need (SEN). This process was thorough but could sometimes be long-winded and bureaucratic. After a process of pilot studies and consultation, provision will be made as part of an Education, Health and Care Plan (EHCP; see later for more details). It is claimed that parents will be given more say in the use of finances to support their child. However, the professional guidance about the best resources may not be as readily available. Cuts to local authority funding and staffing are likely to mean that obtaining really good advice about schooling and suitable interventions may be compromised.

▶ Long-term outcomes for children with ASD

Kanner followed up the children he originally diagnosed and conducted the first longitudinal studies 13 years after his original work. He noted that the children had shown major improvements in terms of language and educational attainments but the key features of social withdrawal and insistence on sameness remained. In the 1980s, a team of researchers from Nottingham University conducted a follow-up study on 100 people diagnosed with ASD in the 1950s and 1960s. They selected subjects who were assessed to have average cognitive abilities. At the follow-up, the majority were living at home with their parents, some were in residential care and some in hospitals. One participant was married. In 2004, Patricia Howlin and her colleagues reported on outcomes for 68 adult subjects, all diagnosed in childhood, who were assessed to be more able. They found that many had continued to make progress since they were seen in childhood. Almost a third were in employment, and around a quarter of the group were described by parents as having some friendships. One-fifth had managed to obtain some qualifications at school and five of these individuals had gone on to college or university, with two studying at postgraduate level. There were four individuals who had married. However, only eight of the group had achieved a high level of independence. The majority remained highly dependent on their families or required some form of residential provision. Howlin also reported a strong correlation between better outcomes and measured intelligence and this is noted in other studies. Children with average and above cognitive abilities tended to do better long term.

It should be noted that many earlier follow-up studies were conducted on people who were diagnosed before the diagnosis of Asperger's syndrome existed. The subjects were those who were predominantly lower functioning.

There is some recent evidence that children with mild ASD and average range ability may see a lessening of symptoms; up to 20 per cent of children may no longer meet the diagnostic criteria as adults, although social and communication difficulties persist. It is likely, therefore, that future research will show variable outcomes.

A note about financial support

Not least of the problems faced by parents of a child with ASD is the extra costs incurred. In the UK, Disability Living Allowance (DLA) is a benefit that is awarded based on mobility and care needs (not based on diagnosis); having a diagnosis of an ASD will not automatically lead to an award. However, many children on the autism spectrum do qualify for DLA. The benefit is split into two parts called 'Mobility' and 'Care'. These are divided again depending on the level of need: there are two levels for mobility (low and high) and three levels for care (low, middle and high). Adult DLA was abolished and replaced by a Personal Independence Payment (PIP) in October 2013.

▶ Challenges for the future

Our knowledge and understanding of ASD over the last 30 years has grown exponentially. The inclusion of verbal children with Asperger's syndrome has widened the spectrum and along with this has come concerns about both the diagnosis of autism and about the heterogeneity of the condition. Without a doubt, over the next 30 years, research into the range of disorders that currently make up ASD will elucidate distinct subtypes. The way forward in such research will be led by improved assessment, MRI scanning and genetic and chromosome analyses. At the same time, the revolution in technology is offering new possibilities to improved interventions. In conclusion, the following unresolved issues are raised as 'crystal ball' speculations:

▶ **Advances in interventions: iPads, AAC**

While the tools technology offer can be useful for anyone, they can be particularly useful for those with limited abilities in language and communication. There are hundreds of apps, web-based tools and technologies to help those with autism communicate and learn. Some focus on one particular skill or task and others encompass a wide array of functionality. They offer children with ASD an alternative way of communicating. In view of the progress made in the last five years in these technologies the prospects are immense.

▶ **Changes in SEN legislation**

In the UK Statements of SEN will be replaced by the EHCP, which will extend statutory protection for children with SEN up to the age of 25 for those in further education. It is unclear how this will affect those who are in non-educational support. The proposed new duty on councils to produce a 'local offer', setting out the support available locally for children with SEN, will help increase transparency for parents. In addition, the legislation will put new duties on local authorities and local health bodies to be more joined-up at a local level and joint commission services. Many parents might not have the information or resources to be able to ensure that there are suitable services that meet their child's needs. It is also unclear how children in Academy Schools will be able to access services. There are concerns about whether the reforms will help improve support for those children who do not have a Statement or EHCP.

▶ Too wide a spectrum that does no one any justice?

The range of children under the ASD umbrella is very wide. At one extreme are children with severe ASD and profound ID and at the other there those who are highly intelligent, well-educated and self-sufficient. The public perception of ASD is influenced by high-profile films and publicity about 'unusual talents', although this is a tiny minority of people with ASD. People with mild symptoms (such as those diagnosed previously with Asperger's syndrome) are dismayed to be labelled as autistic, as was evident by the opposition to DSM-5. Equally, parents of children with severe ASD feel marginalized and concerned that funding is not directed at the most vulnerable. In the interests of both groups this needs to be addressed.

▶ Harmonization of DSM-5 and ICD-11

At present, it is not clear whether ICD-11 will follow the lead given by DSM-5 in subsuming the subgroups under one general diagnosis of ASD. If ICD-11 retains Asperger's syndrome then there will be a very confusing situation of future Asperger's syndrome diagnoses being available in Europe but not in the USA. At the same time, as has been discussed throughout this book, genetic research is identifying various subgroups of ASD. There are two opposing trends: the fragmentation of ASD into various specific subgroups as opposed to the consolidation under one umbrella term, namely ASD. Conceptual confusions of this nature impede research.

▶ The introduction of levels of severity in DSM-5

Although there has always been an implicit assumption that there were levels of severity in ASD, some children being mildly affected and others more so, a confounding factor has been the child's cognitive abilities. Although it is generally the case that there is a high correlation between severity of ASD and degree of ID, there are cases of ASD where the child has been assessed to have high levels of cognitive functioning and is nevertheless severely autistic.

There is a lack of clarity about the three levels of severity in DSM-5 and how they should be applied.

▶ The ethics of genetic investigations – where will it all lead?

Clinicians and parents are on the edge of a precipice with regard to genetic testing with much cheaper and precise techniques available. However, whether we wish to know an individual's genetic inheritance and life-chances when he or she is in infancy opens a Pandora's box of ethical issues.

▶ Improving diagnosis

It is clear that the reliability and validity of diagnostic assessment needs to be improved. Diagnosis needs to be far more thorough and standardized and it should not be a 'postcode lottery'. Diagnosis of ASD could be regarded as the starting point for further investigations. If assessment yielded more reliable data including cognitive abilities, language skills, patterns of onset, co-morbid symptoms and genetic testing then diagnosis could be more specific. This would lead to the possibility of homogeneity in research samples. With a thorough assessment it should be possible to identify subtypes of ASD which will lead to more targeted interventions.

This 100 ideas section gives ways of exploring the subject of ASD in more depth.

100
IDEAS

20 Key Books

1 Vygotsky, L. (1978) *Mind in Society*, Harvard: Harvard University Press.

2 Asperger, H. in Frith, U. (Ed.) (1991) *Autism & Asperger's Syndrome*, Cambridge: CUP.

3 Hansen, R. and Rogers, S. (2013) *Autism and other Neurodevelopmental Disorders*, Washington DC: American Psychiatric Publishing.

4 Baron-Cohen, S. (2010) *Zero Degrees of Empathy*, London: Penguin.

5 Goldstein, S., Nagliari, J. and Ozonoff, S. (2009) *Assessment of Autism Spectrum Disorders,* New York: The Guilford Press.

6 Gardner, H. (2011) *Frames of Mind*, New York: Basic Books.

7 Happé, F. and Frith, U. (eds) (2010) *Autism and Talent. Philosophical Transactions of the Royal Society*, Oxford: OUP.

8 Jordan, R. and Powell, S. (1995) *Understanding and Teaching Children with Autism*, Chichester: John Wiley & Son.

9 Attwood, T. (2007) *The Complete Guide to Asperger's Syndrome*, London, Jessica Kingsley.

10 Mesibov, G., Shea, V. and Schopler, E. (2004) *The TEACCH Approach to Autistic Spectrum Disorders*, New York: Plenum.

11 Walsh, N. and Hurley, E. (2013) *The Good and Bad Science of Autism*, Birmingham: Autism West Midlands.

12 Abrahams, B. and Geschwind, D. (2008) 'Advances in autism genetics: On the threshold of a new neurobiology', *Nature*, **9**, 341–56.

13 Tantam, D. (2009) *Can the World Afford Autistic Spectrum Disorder?*, London: Jessica Kingsley.

14 Baron-Cohen, S. (1997) *Mind Blindness. An essay on Autism and Theory of Mind*, Cambridge, MA Mass.: MIT Press.

15 Frith, U. and Hill, E. (2004) *Autism, Mind and Brain*, Oxford: OUP.

16 Baron-Cohen, S. (2009) Autism: The Empathising-Systemising (ES) Theory, *Ann NY Acad Sci*, 1156, 68–80.

17 Baron-Cohen, S. (2008) *Autism and Asperger's Syndrome, the Facts*, Oxford: OUP.

18 Coleman, M. and Gilberg, C. (2011) *The Autisms* (4th Edition), Oxford: OUP.

19 Wing, L. (2003) *The Autistic Spectrum: a Guide for Parents and Professionals*, London: Constable & Co.

20 Cumine, V., Dunlop, J. and Stevenson, G. (2000) *Autism in the Early Years. A Practical Guide*, London: David Fulton.

10 Charities Working for People with ASD

1 The National Autistic Society (NAS): a British charity for people with ASD. The purpose of the organization is to improve the lives of people with autism in the UK. Founded in 1962 it has around 20,000 members. The NAS is funded through voluntary contributions and charity events. It has the following names registered with the Charity Commission: The National Autistic Society; National Society for Autistic Children; Autism UK; Action for Autism. The National Autistic Society, 393 City Road, London, EC1V 1NG, UK. Tel: +44 (0)20 7833 2299; Fax: +44 (0)20 7833 9666; Email: nas@nas.org.uk; Website: www.autism.org.uk.

2 The National Autistic Society in Scotland, Central Chambers, 1st Floor 109 Hope Street, Glasgow, Scotland. Tel: +44 (0) 141 221 8090; Email: scotland@nas.org.uk; Website: http://www.autism.org.uk/scotland.html.

3 National Autistic Society Cymru, 6–7 Village Way, Greenmeadows, Spring Business Park, Tongwynlais,

Cardiff CF15 7NE, UK. Tel: + 44 (0) 2920 629 312; Email: Cymru@nas.org.uk; Website: http://www. autism.org.uk/cymru.

4 Autism NI (PAPA) Donard House, Knockbracken Healthcare Park, Saintfield Road, Belfast, Northern Ireland. BT8 8BH. Tel: +44 (0) 28 90 401729; Helpline 0845 055 9010; Email: info@autismni.org; Website: http://ww.autismni.org.

5 NORSACA (Nottingham Regional Society for Autistic Children and Adults) Whitegates FE Unit, Park Street, Worksop, S80 1HH, Nottinghamshire, UK Tel: +44 (0) 1909 509400. (NORSACA runs the Elizabeth Newson Assessment facility.) Email: info@norsaca.org.uk; NORSACA Park Hall Autism Resource Centre, Park Road, Bestwood Village, Nottingham, NG6 8TQ. Tel: 0115 976 1805; Website: www.norsaca.org.uk/.

6 Autism West Midlands, Regent Court, George Road, Birmingham, B15 1NU, UK. Email: shop@ autismwestmidlands.org.uk. Tel: 0121 450 7582; Website: www.autismwestmidlands.org.uk/.

7 Autism Initiatives UK: a parent-led charity and a member of both the Autism Alliance and the Confederation of Service Providers for People with Autism (CoSPPA). 7 Chesterfield Road, Liverpool, Merseyside, L23 9XL, UK. Tel: 0151 330 9500; Website: www.autisminitiatives.org/contact-us/.

8 Autistica: founded 2004. Funds medical research to understand the causes of autism, improve diagnosis and develop new treatments and interventions. One of

the UK's leading autism medical research charities. 100a Chalk Farm Road, London, NW1 8EH, UK. Tel: +44 (0) 560 118 360; Email: info@autistica.org.uk; Website: www.autistica.org.uk/.

9 Autism Society of America, 7910 Woodmont Avenue, Suite 300, Bethesda, Maryland 20814, USA. Tel: +1 301 657 0881; Email: info@autism-society.org; Website http://www.autism-society.org.

10 Unique. This is a source of information and support to families and individuals affected by any rare chromosome disorder and to the professionals who work with them. Unique is a UK-based charity but welcomes members worldwide. Membership of Unique is free. PO Box 2189, Caterham, Surrey, CR3 5GN, UK. Tel: +44 (0)1883 330 766; Email: info@rarechromo.org; Website: www.rarechromo.co.uk/.

5 Journals that Report Research on ASD

1 *Journal of Autism and Developmental Disorders*. The leading peer-reviewed periodical focusing on all aspects of ASD and related developmental disabilities.

2 *Focus on Autism and Other Developmental Disabilities.* A journal offering practical educational and treatment suggestions for teachers, trainers and parents.

3 *Autism*. International forum for research of direct and practical relevance to improving the quality of life for those with ASD.

4 *The British Journal of Learning Disabilities.* International peer-reviewed, inter-disciplinary journal. Published by the British Institute of Learning Disability.

5 *Special.* National Association for Special Educational Needs (NASEN). For all professionals and parents of ASD children. It provides up-to-date news in special needs education policy and research.

10 Candidate Genes

Research is identifying mutated genes which appear to increase the risk of having ASD. The table below lists some of these. Every gene is given a code number. Its location in the chromosome is also identified by a coding system. Data relating to the findings of geneticists are given in the description column with regard to the significance of the gene for ASD.

Gene	Location	Description
NRXN1 Neurexin	2q32	In 2007, researchers in the Autism Genome Project (an international research team composed of 137 scientists in 50 institutions) reported that aberrations of a brain-development gene, neurexin 1, could be involved in some cases of autism. These genes are particularly active very early in brain development. DNA was obtained from 1,181 families in the largest-scale genome scan conducted in autism research at the time.
RELN Reelin	7q22	The Reelin gene plays a vital role in cell migration processes acting as a stop signal for migrating neurons in the brain. Post-mortem studies of people with ASD have found evidence of altered neuronal migration.

MET	7q31	Several studies have shown that mutations in MET appear more frequently in people with autism than in controls. MET influences the strength of connections between brain regions involved in social behaviours.
CNTNAP2	7q35-q36	Multiple studies have identified that the CNTNAP2 gene is implicated in autism. It encodes a cell adhesion protein that regulates signalling between neurons at the synapse and is known to be involved in language development. Disrupting the gene's activity may impair synapse formation.
GABRB3	Multiple and 15q11	Rare variants in the GABRB3 gene have been identified as being involved with autism and childhood absence epilepsy. The gene encodes a protein known to be involved in inhibiting neural transmission in the brain. The GABRB3 gene has also been associated with autistic savant skills.
CACNA1G	17q22	The CACNA1G is a gene which appears to be involved in neurotransmission involving calcium. Evidence implicating mutations in calcium channel genes in ASD has been accumulating.
SHANK3	22q13	The SHANK3 gene provides instructions for making a protein that is found in many of the body's tissues but is most abundant in the brain. It plays a role in the functioning of synapses, which are the connections between nerve cells (neurons) where cell-to-cell communication occurs. Researchers believe that a reduction in the amount of SHANK3 protein is responsible for many of the features of ASD.
MECP2	Xq28	Recent genetic studies have shown that two similar neurodevelopmental disorders, Rett's syndrome and autism, are linked to a mutation in the MECP2 gene which is found on the X chromosome. Mutations on the MECP2 gene are also known to cause other post-natal neuro-developmental disorders.

ALL THAT MATTERS: ASD

NLGN3 NLGN4X Neuroligins	Xq13	Some studies have reported mutations in two X-linked genes, neuroligins NLGN3 and NLGN4, in children with ASD. Mutations appear to affect cell adhesion molecules at the synapse and suggest that a defect in these may predispose a child to autism.	
OXTR	3p25	Evidence both from animal and human studies suggests that mutations in the oxytocin receptor gene are likely candidates conferring a risk of ASD. Recent human studies have shown that administration of oxytocin modulates social behaviour.	

This information has largely been gathered from www. sfari.org.uk.

10 Candidate Chromosome Abnormalities

Changes in the structure of the chromosomes have been found to be related to a wide range of disabilities including ASD. The following table is a list of some of the chromosome variations known to be implicated. The first column gives the chromosome number; the second the type of aberration identified; the third lists the degree of learning disability associated with the aberrations; and the last column shows reported cases of ASD.

Chromosome number	Aberration	Associated learning difficulties	ASD reported in more than 25% of known cases
1	Deletions, duplications and supernumerary ring	ID mild-severe	Autistic-like behaviours
2	Deletions	ID moderate-severe	ASD
5	Deletions	ID variable	ASD

7	Deletions, duplications and translocations	ID mild – moderate	ASD
11	Deletions	ID mild-moderate	ASD in 45% of cases
15	Deletions and duplications	ID mild	ASD traits common
16	Deletions and duplications	ID variable	ASD in 50–70% of cases.
17	Deletions and duplications	ID mild– moderate	ASD in 75% cases
22	Ring (SHANK 3 gene)	ID moderate-severe	ASD
23	Duplications	ID variable	ASD traits

5 Sources for Suitable Toys, Equipment and Activities

1 NAS Early Bird Team provides a helpful list of suggestions. These include: use of coloured torches; a marble run; toy trains; a jack in the box; trampoline; ball pool; rocking horse/chair; and sensory stimulation such as twinkling lights and kaleidoscopes (www.autism.org.uk).

2 Books for fun: Thomas the Tank Engine, Mr Men and Dr Seuss series.

3 Software and DVDs: e.g. The Transporters (www.transporters.tv), Jump Ahead Toddler series. Focus Multimedia Ltd.

4 Games teaching co-operation: Picture Lotto, Snap, Ludo, Snakes and Ladders, Noughts and Crosses, Connect 4, Chess.

5 Specialist equipment for sensory stimulation can be obtained from a company such as TFH5-7 Severnside Business Park, Stourport-on-Severn, Worcestershire, DY13 9HT, UK. Tel: 01299 827820; Email: info@specialneedstoys.com.

5 Books Offering Support and Practical Advice

1 *Managing Asperger Syndrome at College and University: A Resource for Students, Tutors and Support Services*, Jamieson, J. & C. (2004).

2 *Autism and Asperger Syndrome: Preparing for Adulthood*. Howlin, P. (2004).

3 *It's Raining Cats and Dogs: An Autism Spectrum Guide to the Confusing World of Idioms, Metaphors and Everyday Expressions*. Barton, M. (2012).

4 *My Brother is Different: A Book for Young Children Who Have a Brother or Sister with Autism*. Garrod, L. (2000).

5 *Teaching Children to Mind-Read: a Practical Guide*. Howlin, P., Baron-Cohen, S. and Hadwin, J. (1999).

5 Documentary Films About ASD

1 *Autism: The Musical* (2007). The film follows five Los Angeles children over the course of six months, capturing their struggles and triumphs.

2 *The Horse Boy* (2009). Chronicles the journey of a family as they travel through Mongolia in search of a

mysterious shaman who they believe can heal their autistic son.

3 *Her Name is Sabine* (2008). The director, using her own video archive and shooting new material herself, offers a moving story about her sister Sabine, who has autism.

4 *After Thomas* (2006). A true story of a child with severe autism whose parents get a Labrador pup to provide a key to solve his problems forming relationships. But more complications follow to threaten his progress.

5 *A is for Autism* (YouTube) (1992). An animated film using autistic savant art with the voices of ASD children explaining their feelings, concerns and ideas.

5 Films of Fictional Accounts of ASD (apart from *Rain Man*)

1 *I Am Sam* (1998). Stars: Sean Penn and Michele Pfeiffer. The story of an autistic man living independently and functioning well until he becomes a father and has to care for his small child.

2 *Little Man Tate* (1991). Director: Jodie Foster. The story of a highly talented child with many Asperger's traits, whose mother is determined to protect him from opportunists wishing to exploit his talents.

3 *Snow Cake* (2006). Stars: Alan Rickman and Sigourney Weaver. A drama about a middle-aged woman with autism and the friendship she develops with a man who is traumatized after a car accident.

4 *The Boy Who Could Fly* (1986). Stars: Jay Underwood. A teenager with autism is sent to live with a relative after the death of his parents. He is befriended by a girl living next door.

5 *Adam* (2009). Stars: Amy Irvin. A romantic drama, in which a boy with Asperger's syndrome tries to develop a romantic relationship with a girl who is not on the spectrum.

5 Autobiographical Accounts

1 *Emergence: Labelled Autistic*, by Temple Grandin and Margaret M. Scariano (2005).

2 *Born on a Blue Day: Inside the Extraordinary Mind of an Autistic Savant*, by Daniel Tammet (2007).

3 *My World is Not Your Worl'd* by Alison Hale (1998).

4 *Freaks, Geeks and Asperger's Syndrome*, by Luke Jackson (2002).

5 *Nobody Nowhere* by Donna Williams (1992).

5 Celebrated Autistic Savants

Savant syndrome is a condition in which people with ASD have prodigious talents in excess of what is considered normal in specific areas such as rapid calculation, art, memory or musical skills. While they have low scores on IQ tests they have abilities beyond those of similar age in the normal population. This 'syndrome' is not recognized as a mental disorder in the ICD-10 or the DSM-5.

1 Nadia was born in 1967. She had severe learning difficulties yet from the age of three drew pictures of fairground horses with astonishing skill. She bypassed all the usual rules for the development of drawing ability in children. By the age of five she had a repertoire of subjects, mainly animals, which she drew rapidly and fluently, preferably in biro. Her work became of international interest encouraging investigation into other savants. Nadia had no communicative speech and was excessively slow in her movements: fine and gross motor development was delayed. She could not dress herself or manage a knife and fork. By the age of 12 her ability to draw petered out. In 2013 she was living in a specialist care home. Her wonderful pictures adorn the walls of the hallway where she lives, but she shows no interest in them. She spends her days totally dependent on others. (See: Selfe, L. (2011) *Nadia Revisited*).

2 Derek Paravacini has remarkable musical ability, performing internationally in 2013. He was born totally blind, with severe developmental and learning disabilities. Derek requires 24-hour care and support but his ability as a musician transcends his disabilities. His talent is such that he can perform a piece of music on request and change the style in which it is played, as jazz, swing, syncopation, classical or other suggested form. He has played with great success in clubs and concert halls in the UK and the USA. (See: Ockelford, A. (2006) *In the Key of Genius*).

3 Stephen Wiltshire was born in London in 1974. His remarkable art work has been monitored from his

earliest years. In early childhood he had no language and did not interact with others. At the age of three he was diagnosed as being autistic. Two years later he entered a school where his drawing skills were first observed and encouraged. By the age of nine he was drawing complex city views of buildings, roads and traffic. He had mastered perspective in a dramatic way and his memory for detail after comparatively brief periods of observation enabled him to produce drawings of exceptional realism. (See Wiltshire, S. (1991) *Floating Cities*).

4 Kim Peek (1951–2009) was born with severe brain damage but was known to have read and memorized over a thousand books. He was the inspiration for the film *Rain Man*. He had an IQ below 80, had problems with basic motor skills, walking, doing up buttons, catching, throwing and writing. However, he demonstrated an encyclopaedic knowledge of geography, music and literature. In 2008 a study concluded that he had a rare genetic syndrome resulting in physical anomalies, including low muscle tone and an abnormally large head. (See Treffert, D. (1989) *Extraordinary People*).

5 Christopher, born in the 1960s, was placed in a school for disabled children. His mother had contracted rubella in pregnancy. From the age of three he showed interest in language, picking up some French from his sister's textbooks. While at 14 his verbal IQ score was the average normal (just below 100) it was well below that for perceptual, spatial abilities. Although he was unable to lead an independent life, by his mid-

30s he could understand, speak, write and translate from 16 languages. He could not understand jokes or other people's states of mind. (See Hermelin, B. (2001) *Bright Splinters of the Mind*).

5 Stories about ASD for Adults

1 *Daniel Isn't Talking*, by Marti Leimbach (2011). A moving story of a family in crisis, told with warmth, compassion and humour.

2 *A Rock and A Hard Place*, by Anne Sutcliffe (2006). A mother's account of coping with a severely autistic daughter whose behaviour is destructive.

3 *Tilt*, by Elizabeth Burns (2004). How a woman reassesses her life and motherhood when confronted with her oldest daughter's severe autism.

4 *Confidential Sources*, by Barbara Fischkin (2006). A book that deals with journalism, love and family life, in which there is a child with ASD. The NAS was consulted regarding the issues of autism.

5 *The Curious Incident of the Dog in the Night-time*, by Mark Haddon (2003). A bright young man with Asperger's syndrome uses his unique approach to solve a crime.

5 Stories about ASD for Children

1 *Blue Bottle Mystery: An Asperger Adventure*, by Kathy Hoopmann (2000). Age range: seven and over. A fantasy story for children with a difference; the hero is a boy with Asperger's syndrome.

2 *Taking Autism to School,* by Andreanna Edwards (2002). Age range: three and over. A story of how Angel learns about her classmate Sam's autistic behaviour.

3 *Rules,* by Cynthia Lord (2009). Age range: nine to twelve. Catherine's brother has autism. He has confusion about following social rules. The book examines the problems of feeling different and it is her own behaviour that makes her ask, 'What is normal?'

4 *Something Different About Dad: How to Live With Your Asperger's Parent,* by Kirsti Evans (2011). Growing up with a parent on the autistic spectrum can leave children feeling confused and worried. Two children learn to cope with their father's Asperger's syndrome.

5 *Ian's Walk: A Story about Autism*, an illustrated book by Laurie Lears (2003). Age range: four to eight. Autism is seen through the eyes of the young boy's older sister.

5 Arts-based Therapies for Children with ASD

1 **Music therapy:** has been shown to be beneficial for people with ASD. It can reduce stress, promote communication and enhance social interaction. Unfortunately, provision is patchy. Therapists must complete a postgraduate accredited course recognized by the Health and Care Professions Council. More information can be obtained from Introduction to Music Therapy: Information Pack at www.musicatwork.co.uk.

Theatres are beginning to cater for children on the autistic spectrum with 'relaxed performances' where they can feel comfortable. Researchers have used drama games to promote empathy, improvisation and perspective shifting.

2 **The Red Kite Project – Autism Documentary (DVD):** The artistic director of Chicago Children's Theatre creates the first interactive, multi-sensory theatrical performance installation for autistic children.

3 **University of Kent (UK):** Programmes have been devised showing developments in the ways theatre can encourage those with ASD to join in. Comic performances can promote communication and interaction for children who participate with shouts, whistles and cries at dramatic moments.

4 **Oxford Playhouse (UK):** 'Relaxed performances' for children with ASD have been devised which means that a blind eye is turned to any disruptive behaviour: children can move around; actors are prepared for audience movement and noise during the performance. In London 'autistic friendly' productions of Disney's *The Lion King* have taken place.

5 **The Autism Matters Theatre** (UK): in partnership with Research Autism provides a mixture of latest news and research, in-depth talks, high-profile speakers and lunchtime entertainment.

Further reading

Chapter 1

1 Parris, M. August 17th, 2013, *The Times*, p. 21.
2 Thatcher, M. October 31, 1987, talking to *Women's Own*.
3 Vygotsky, L. (1978). *Mind in Society*, Harvard: Harvard University Press.
4 Wittgenstein, L. (2009). *Philosophical Investigations*, Oxford: Wiley Blackwell.
5 Itard, J.M.G. (1962). *The Wild Boy of Aveyron* (G. Humphrey and M. Humphrey, Trans.) New York: Appleton-Century-Crofts.
6 Coleman, M. and Gillberg, C. (2011). *The Autisms*, Oxford: OUP.

Chapter 2

7 Goldstein, S., Nagliari, J. and Ozonoff, S. (2009). *Assessment of Autism Spectrum Disorders,* New York: The Guilford Press.
8 Kanner, L. (1943). 'Autistic disturbances of affective contact', *Nervous Child*, 2, 217–250.
9 Asperger, H. in Frith, U. (Ed) (1991). *Autism and Asperger's Syndrome*, Cambridge: CUP.
10 Frith, U. (See 9 above).
11 Wing, L. and Gould, J. (1979). 'Severe impairments of social interaction and associated abnormalities in children: Epidemiology and classification', *Journal of Autism and Developmental Disorders*, 9, 11–29.
12 Hansen, R. and Rogers, S. (2013). *Autism and Other Neurodevelopmental Disorders*, Washington DC: American Psychiatric Publishing.
13 Shattuck, P. (2006). 'The contribution of diagnostic substitution to the growing administrative prevalence of autism in US Special Education', *Pediatrics*, 117, 1028–37.
14 Goldstein, S. (See 7 above).

Chapter 3

15 Baron-Cohen, S. (2011). *Zero Degrees of Empathy*, Harmondsworth: Penguin.
16 Dr James Scully, Medical Director of the APA (2008). Autism and Other Pervasive Developmental Disorders Conference. www.dsm5.org/research.
17 Huerta, M., Somer, L., Bishop, P. et al. (2012). 'Application of DSM-5 criteria for autism spectrum disorder to three samples of children with DSM-4 diagnoses of PDD', *American Journal of Psychiatry*, 169,1056–1064.
18 National Autistic Society: website: www.autism.org.uk.
19 Green, H., June 2013, *The Psychologist.*, p.382.

Chapter 4

20 Nagliari, J. and Chambers, K. (2009). 'Psychometric issues and current scales' (See 7 above).

21 Gardner, H. (2011). *Frames of Mind*, New York: Basic Books.

22 Rutter, M., Le Couter, A. and Lord, C. (2004). *Autism Diagnostic Interview* (Revised), Los Angeles Western Psychological Services.

23 Lord, C., Rutter, M., Goode, S. et al. (1989). *Autism Diagnostic Observation Schedule*, London: Hogrefe.

24 Wing, L. and Gould, J. (1991). *Diagnostic Instrument for Social Communication Disorder*, Bromley: Eliot House.

25 Skuse, D., Warrington, R., Bishop, D. et al. (2004). 'The development, diagnostic and dimensional interview (3di): a novel computerized assessment for autism spectrum disorders', *Journal of the American Academy of Child and Adolescent Psychiatry*, 43 (5), 548–58.

26 Happé, F., Ronald, A. and Plomin, R. (2006). 'Time to give up a single cause for autism', *Nature Neuroscience*, 9, (10), 1218–20.

27 Howlin, P., Goode, S., Hutton, J. and Rutter, M. (2009). 'Savant skills in autism psychometric approaches and parental reports'. In F. Happé and U. Frith. (Eds) *Autism and Talent; Philosophical Transactions of the Royal Society*, Oxford: OUP.

28 Klin, A. (2009). 'Subtyping the Autism Spectrum Disorder' (See 7 above).

29 Lovaas, I. (1987). 'Behavioural treatment and normal educational and intellectual functioning in young autistic children', *Journal of Consulting and Clinical Psychology*, 55 (1), 3–9.

30 Naoki, H. (2013). *The Reason I Jump*, London: Hodder and Stoughton.

31 Baron-Cohen, S. (2008). *Autism and Asperger's Syndrome, the Facts*, Oxford: OUP.

32 Kogan, M., Blumberg, S., Schieve, H. et al. (2009). 'Prevalence of parent reported diagnosis of autistic spectrum disorder among children in the US', *Paediatrics*, 124, 1395–1403 (An American Government research project).

33 Pilgrim, D. (2000). 'Psychiatric diagnosis – More questions than answers?', *The Psychologist*, 13 (6), 302–305.

34 Aitken, K. (2010). *The A-Z of Genetics in Autism: A Guide for Professionals*, London: Jessica Kingsley.

35 Timini, S. Gardner, N. and McCabe, B. (2010). *The Myth of Autism,* London: Palgrave.

Chapter 5

36 Jordan, R. and Powell, S. (1995). *Understanding and Teaching Children with Autism*, Chichester: John Wiley & Son.

37 Kaufman, B. (1979). *Son Rise; The Miracle Continues*, New York: Kramer.

38 James, W. (1891). *Principles of Psychology*, London: Macmillan, p. 488.

Chapter 6

39 Hewett, D. and Nind, M. (1998). *Interaction in Action*. London: David Fulton Press.

40 Bondy, A. and Frost, L. (1994). *The Picture Exchange Communication System*, Pyramid Educational Consultants.

41 Mesibov, G., Shea, V. and Schopler, E. (2004). *The TEACCH Approach to Autistic Spectrum Disorders*, New York: Plenum.

42 Gray, C. (2010). *Social Stories. The New Social Story Book*, Michigan: Future Horizons Inc.

43 Gray, C. (1997). *Pictures of Me. Introducing students with ASD to their talents, personality and diagnosis*, http://www.thegraycentre.org/bookstore.

44 Rinaldi, W. (1992). *Social Use of Language Programmes*, http://www.wendyrinaldi.com.

45 Spence, S. (1995). *Social Skills Training. Enhancing Social Competence with Children and Adolescents*, Slough: NFER/Nelson.

Chapter 7

46 Barratt, P., Joy, H., Potter, M., Thomas, G. and Whittaker, P. (1998). 'Children with autism and peer group support', *British Journal of Special Education*, **25** (2), (Circle of Friends).

Chapter 9

47 Walsh, N. and Hurley, E. (2013). *The Good and Bad Science of Autism*, Birmingham: Autism West Midlands.

48 Bettelheim, B. (1967). *The Empty Fortress: Infantile Autism & the Birth of the Self*, NY: The Free Press.

49 Rutter, M., Anderson-Wood, L., Beckett, C. et al. (1999). 'Quasi autistic patterns following early global privation', *Journal of Child Psychology and Psychiatry*, **40**, 537–49.

50 Baron-Cohen, S. (2011). (See 15 above).

51 Atladottir, H., Thorsen, P., Ostergaard, L. et al. (2010). 'Maternal infection requiring hospitalization during pregnancy and autism spectrum disorders', *Journal of Autism Developmental Disorders*, **40**, 1423–30.

52 Goldberg, M. (2011). *The Myth of Autism: How a Misunderstood Epidemic is Destroying Our Children*, California: Skyhorse Publishing.

53 Abrahams, B. and Geschwind, D. (2008). 'Advances in autism genetics: On the threshold of a new neurobiology', *Nature*, **9**, 341–56.

54 Coleman, M. and Gilberg, C. (2011). *The Autisms*, (4th Edition) Oxford: OUP.

55 SFARI (www.sfari.org.uk) (Simons Foundation Autism Research Initiatives).

56 Courchesne, E. and Pierce, K. (2005). 'Brain growth in autism during a critical time in development', *International Journal of Developmental Neuroscience*, **23**, 153–70.

57 Casanova, M. and Trippe, J. (2009). 'Radial cytoarchitecture and patterns of cortical connectivity in autism', (see 26 above).

58 Tantam, D (2009). *Can the World Afford Autistic Spectrum Disorder?*, London: Jessica Kingsley.

59 Rizzolatti, G., Fadiga, L. and Galles, G. et al. (1996). 'Premotor cortex and the recognition of motor actions', *Cognitive Brain Research*, **3**, 131–41.

60 Baron-Cohen, S. (2009). 'Autism, the Empathising-Systemising (ES) Theory', Annals of the New York Academy of Sciences.

61 Ecker, C., Marquand, A., Miranda, J. et al. (2010). 'Magnetic resonance imaging-assisted diagnosis of autism spectrum disorder using a multiparameter classification approach', *The Journal of Neuroscience*, 30 (32), 10612–23.

Chapter 10

62 Lawrence, C. (2010). *Explaining Autism Spectrum Disorder*, Emerald Publishing.

63 Wimmer, H. and Perner, J. (1983). 'Beliefs about beliefs: representation and constraining function of wrong beliefs in young children's understanding of deception', *Cognition*, **13**, 103–128.

64 Baron-Cohen, S. (1997). *Mind Blindness. An essay on Autism and Theory of Mind*, Cambridge: MIT Press.

65 Frith, U. and Happé, F. (2001). 'Autism: Beyond Theory of Mind', *Cognition*, **50**, 115–132.

66 Frith, U. and Hill, E. (2004). *Autism, Mind and Brain*, Oxford: OUP.

67 Baron-Cohen, S. (2009), (see 60 above).

68 Baron-Cohen, S., Ashwin, E., Ashwin, C. et al. (2011). 'Talent in autism: Hyper-systemising, hyper-attention to detail and sensory hyper-sensitivity'.

69 Happé , F. and Frith, U. (2006). 'The weak coherence account: Detail focus, cognitive style in autism spectrum disorders', *Journal of Autism and Developmental Disorders*, **35** (1), 5–25.

70 Shah, A. and Frith, U. (1993). 'Why do autistic individuals show superior performance on the block design test?', *Journal of Child Psychology and Psychiatry*, **34**, 1351–64.

71 Happé, F. (1996). 'Studying weak central coherence at low levels: children with autism do not succumb to visual illusions', *Journal of Child Psychology and Psychiatry*, 37 (7), 873–7.

72 Selfe, L. (2011). *Nadia Revisited: A Longitudinal Study of an Autistic Savant*, London: The Psychology Press.

73 Ozonoff, S., Pennington, B. and Rogers, S. (1991). 'Executive function deficits in high functioning autistic individuals', *Journal of Child Psychology and Psychiatry*, **32** (7), 1081–1105.

74 Hill, E. (2004). 'Evaluating the theory of executive dysfunction in autism', *Developmental Review*, **24**, 189–233.

75 Tantam, D. (2009). (See 58 above).

Chapter 11

76 Pellicano, E. and Stears, M. (2011). 'Bridging autism, science and society: Moving towards an ethically informed approach to autism research', *Autism Research*, **4**, 271–82.

Acknowledgements

Writing a short, succinct book is unexpectedly difficult. 'Not that the story need be long but it takes a long time to make it short'. First of all I would like to thank all those people with autism and their parents with whom I have worked down the years for allowing me to share your joys and woes. Being a child psychologist has been an enormous privilege. I would like to thank the members of my family, Amy and Jessie and also Max Bayley, for their support and encouragement throughout the process, and especially my husband Paul. Some psychologist friends have given me invaluable advice on the manuscript, especially, Terri Hall, Lynn Stow, Margaret and Nick Oke. My 'man on the Clapham omnibus' is Alan Mack, many thanks to you. I am also indebted to the generous and expert advice of Dr Elisabeth Hurley of Autism West Midlands and Dr Beverly Searle of Unique, although any errors are all my own.

Image credits

Photograph of Leo Kanner © Alan Mason/Chesney Medical Archives. Illustration of human chromosomes © Alila Medical Media/Shutterstock.com. Illustration of block designs from Hermelin, B, (2001) *Bright Splinters of the Mind*, Jessica Kingsley. Horse drawing by Lorna Selfe.

Index